*Reports
after the Fire*

Pietro De Marchi

Reports after the Fire

Selected Poems

*translated from Italian by
Peter Robinson*

Shearsman Books

First published in the United Kingdom in 2022 by
Shearsman Books Ltd
PO Box 4239
Swindon
SN3 9FN

Shearsman Books Ltd Registered Office
30–31 St. James Place, Mangotsfield, Bristol BS16 9JB
(this address not for correspondence)

ISBN 978-1-84861-798-8

Translation copyright © 2022 by Peter Robinson
Original poems copyright © Pietro De Marchi, 1999, 2006, 2016, 2022
Introduction and Editorial Matter © 2022 by Peter Robinson

Pietro De Marchi's three poetry collections are published by Edizioni Casagrande, Bellinzona, Switzerland. We are grateful to Edizioni Casagrande for permission to publish the translations contained in this volume and to print the original Italian texts.

Poems from the section containing uncollected work first appeared in the following places: 'L'ignoto di Waterloo', 'Notifiche dopo l'incendio', 'Lezione di scrittura' and 'Il faggio di mio padre' in *LEA – Lingue e letterature d'Oriente e d'Occidente*, no. 6 (2017), pp. 15-16; 'Parlare a una statua' in *Poeti per Vincenzo Vela*, ed. Gianna A. Mina (Bellinzona: Casagrande, 2020), p. 57; 'Su una fotografia di Emmy Andriesse' in *rampe di lancio doganieri nuvole. Omaggio ad Alberto Nessi*, ed. Casa della Letteratura per la Svizzera italiana (Bellinzona: Edizioni Sottoscala, 2020), p. 30; 'Caschi pure il mondo' in *Fanciulle su un muretto* di Giorgio Orelli e *Caschi pure il mondo* di Pietro De Marchi, con un'incisione calcografica di Loredana Müller (Camorino (Canton Ticino): Edizione Areapangeart, 2021).

CONTENTS

Introduction:
Pietro De Marchi and the Lombard Line   8

Note on the Translations   19

Da *Parabole smorzate* (1999) / From *Stunned Parables*

24	Parabole smorzate / Stunned Parables	25
26	Capriccio / Capriccio	27
28	Non lontano da dove / Not Far from Where	29
30	Con Valentina, dalle anatre / With Valentina, at the Ducks	31
32	Una pagina di cielo / A Page of Sky	33
34	Immaginate una coppia… / Imagine a couple…	35
36	Rettili / Reptiles	37
38	Foto di paesaggio con figure / Landscape Photo with Figures	39
40	Verso Marina / Towards Marina	41
42	Lisbona, Rua Garrett / Lisbon, Rua Garrett	43
44	All'angolo di Freiestrasse / At the Corner of Freiestrasse	45
46	Frontespizio / Frontispiece	47
48	Il cigno e l'altalena / The Swan and the Swing	49
50	Gabbiani e folaghe / Seagulls and Coots	51
52	Promesse da marinaio / Promises from Sailors	53
54	Rime baciate / Kissing Rhymes	55
56	Poesia d'amore / Love Poems	57
58	Spiaggia libera / Free Beach	59

Da *Replica* (2006) / From *Reply*

62	Inganno ottico / Trompe l'œil	63
64	Una sovrapposizione per Giampiero Neri / An Overlay for Giampiero Neri	65
66	Lettera da Binz / Letter from Binz	67
68	Davanti alla Pinacoteca / In Front of the Art Museum	69
70	Anni Settanta / The Seventies	71
72	Attraversando la Polonia / Crossing Poland	73

74	Promemoria da un luogo di betulle /	
	Memo from a Place of Birches	75
76	Funerale a Baar / Funeral at Baar	77
78	Qui e non altrove / Here and not Elsewhere	79
80	Variazioni su un tema antico / Variations on an Old Theme	81
82	Diario d'Irlanda / Ireland Diary	83
86	Su una sosia / On a Double	87
88	*Pour prendre congé* / To Take Leave	89
90	Biciclette, generazioni / Bicycles, Generations	91
92	Ancora verso Marina / Once more towards Marina	93
94	In bocca di mare / Facing the Sea	95
96	Cena con geco, a Montepescali /	
	Supper with Gecko, at Montepescali	97
98	Leggendo la segnaletica stradale / Reading the Road-signs	99
100	Come l'acqua / Like Water	101

Da *La carta delle arance* (2016) / From *The Oranges' Paper*

104	Un paesaggio invernale / A Winter Landscape	105
108	Luoghi da rivisitare / Places to Revisit	109
110	Di un cavallo e di un carro / Of a Horse and Cart	111
112	Inventario del Bagno «Rosanna» / "Rosanna" Bathing Inventory	113
114	Madrigale per A. / Madrigal for A.	115
116	Più rapida del desiderio / Quicker than Desire	117
118	Graffiti / Graffiti	119
120	Gente che parla / People who Speak	121
122	Lettera da Zurigo / Letter from Zurich	123
124	Nel paese delle fiabe / In the Land of Fairytales	125
126	La vicina / The Neighbour Woman	127
128	Il disincanto e la metrica / Disillusion and Meter	129
130	Momento di tregua / A Moment's Truce	131
132	Lingue in transito / Languages in Transit	133
134	Rondò di Castelsardo / Castelsardo Rondo	135
136	Per un amatore di gatti / For a Cat Lover	137
138	Viaggiando verso il Monferrato /	
	Journeying towards Montferrat	139
140	Il cielo di maggio in Lombardia / May-time Sky in Lombardy	141

142	Il poeta e il mecenate / The Poet and Maecenas	143
144	Panchine allo zoo / Benches at the Zoo	145
146	Augenlicht / Eyesight	147
150	La casa di Keats / Keats' House	151
152	Un posto così / Such a Place	153
154	Charlot / Charlie	155
156	Una delle dieci / One of the Ten	157
158	Ipotesi sull'ultimo sogno / Surmises about the Last Dream	159
160	La carta delle arance / The Oranges' Paper	161

Inediti (2021) / Uncollected

164	L'ignoto di Waterloo / The Unknown Soldier of Waterloo	165
166	Lezione di scrittura / Writing Lesson	167
168	Notifiche dopo l'incendio / Reports after the Fire	169
170	Il faggio di mio padre / My Father's Beech Tree	171
172	Parlare a una statua / Speaking to a Statue	173
174	Su una fotografia di Emmy Andriesse / On a Photo by Emmy Andriesse	175
176	Le case, le cose / The Houses, the Things	177
178	Come la pantera di Rilke / Like Rilke's Panther	179
180	Finale di partita / End of Game	181
182	Caschi pure il mondo / Go Let the World Tumble	183

Notes	184

INTRODUCTION

PIETRO DE MARCHI AND THE LOMBARD LINE

Evoking W. H. Auden's 'Musée des Beaux Arts' in epigraphs for two of his poems, the Swiss-based Italian poet Pietro De Marchi tests on his pulses aspects of the British poet's insights about human perspectives and pain, and of pain figured in artistic representation. The earlier of these is 'Davanti alla Pinacoteca' ('In Front of the Art Museum'), which uses a snippet to orientate readers by picking out the tiny detail that the suffering about which the old Masters were never wrong in Auden's poem 'takes place / While someone else is eating':

> Sat at a table in the corner bar
> between Brera and Fiori Chiari
> you watch and listen to the daily life.
> There's those who tell their own and others' stories,
> stories of children, of husbands and wives.
> There's those who explain the Golden Section
> because they have an exam this afternoon
> and still they don't get it.
> When a boy goes by dressed a bit like an artist,
> a girl turns and says, shit!, I'm falling in love.
> Her mobile goes off at that moment: it's her mother,
> she's heard it on the radio.
> There's those at another table who are informed:
> yes, bombs, this morning, on the London Underground.
> There's those who arrive only now and know nothing,
> they settle down, glance at the menu, order then
> white wine, melon and Parma ham.

Among the themes that this poem addresses, it might be said, is that in art things cannot be said once and for all, even when they are said definitively by classic poets, for the times move on, and the circumstances change so that it is possible to think that we have overcome the problems of earlier societies. Yet, if anything, the predicament identified in the Brussels art museum late in 1938 has intensified with the developments in communication technology between then and 5 July 2005. The ploughman in Breughel's painting is both too busy and too far away to see Icarus's legs about to disappear beneath the waves in the middle distance, and there's nothing he could have done to help. Nor could the ship that 'sailed calmly on' have been able to redirect the wind to reach the mythological son of Dedalus and save him from his fate.

But the girl in De Marchi's poem has a mobile phone and finds out about the London bombings the same morning that they happen. How is human feeling and ethical attention to cope with the simultaneous coexistence of cruel, tragic, and pleasurable experiences. Given the short attention spans of contemporary existence, 'distracted from distraction by distraction', as T. S. Eliot put it in *Burnt Norton*, and the globally consumerised demands on individuals in our attention economy, it is down to the poets of every generation to relate themselves both to things past, and passing, and to come, and to remind us in their own terms of whatever it might feel essential for cultures to remember.

We can see this in De Marchi's poems that delicately touch on the fate of the Jews in Europe, and how they rise to the challenges articulated in, for example, Geoffrey Hill's 'September Song' as well as poems by Franco Fortini and Vittorio Sereni, or the poetry and prose of Giorgio Bassani and Primo Levi. Alongside its epigraphs and dedications, De Marchi's poetry is allusively aware of its inheritances and indebtednesses. These it can signal overtly, as in the epigraph to the final section of *Replica*, which is called 'L'estate' and evokes its theme by citing the phrase 'come di là dal valico un ritorno d'estate' ('like a summer's return from the far side of the pass') from Vittorio Sereni's 'Autostrada della Cisa' in *Stella variabile*, or it can be done tacitly, as when in the second section of 'Centerville, Iowa' (not included in this selection), immediately after the mention of Ellis Island, silently De Marchi cites 'con tutta quell'America davanti' ('with all of that America before them') which appears in the third part of 'Lavori in corso' ('Works in Progress') from that same poet's 1981 collection.

As we know from Walter Jackson Bate's *The Burden of the Past and the English Poet* (1970) and its psychologically agonistic successor *The Anxiety of Influence: A Theory of Poetry* (1973) by Harold Bloom, being a late arrival in a distinguished tradition is also a predicament. De Marchi's poetry manifests at least three effective ways of overcoming the potentially silencing burden and angst of having such distinctive forebears as Eugenio Montale, Vittorio Sereni and Luciano Erba. These are a willingness to learn from predecessors, and the cultural memory that this requires, a readiness to acknowledge debts and to celebrate them with gratitude, and a determination to draw upon and articulate one's own intuitions, insights, and materials – which are inevitably those of his generation in its times. It is thus that, in the second poem that alludes to Auden's 'Musée des Beaux Arts', the background details from *Winter Landscape with Massacre of the Innocents* by Marten Van Cleve also 'will want to say something'.

Pietro De Marchi was born in Seregno, near Milan, in 1958. His family has roots in both Lombardy and the Veneto, and while his father was, as poems selected and translated here indicate more than once, a voracious reader and the poet grew up in a house of books, the employment of his male relatives included coal-mining and working for Pirelli, whose factory, the Bicocca, near where they lived, included an entire neighbourhood of Milan constructed to house its workers. De Marchi's familiarity with the two great classics of the Italian educational system, Dante's *Divina commedia* and Manzoni's *I promessi sposi*, as well as with the strong and unbroken tradition of Italian poetry from Leopardi to the present day began early and led him towards literature as the subject for his university degree.

After graduating from the University of Milan he crossed the border into Switzerland, going to Zurich to study for his doctorate. Since 1984 he has lived and worked in that most international of Swiss cities, teaching Italian literature at the university there, as well as giving classes at Neuchâtel and Bern. These briefest details of the poet's biography help explain some of the epigraphs and dedications that orientate a reader as regards his poetic affections and loyalties; and they might be described, with a certain equivocal irony, as prolonging and extending the Swiss branch of the *Linea Lombarda*, the Lombard Line of poets. But before we get to what such a set of allegiances might mean, there are also implications to be drawn from the poet growing up in Northern Italy in the second half of the 1950s.

Those born around the middle of the twentieth century in the industrial cities of Europe experienced forms of a society on the point of rapidly disorientating transition, and found themselves on the juvenile side of the first generation gap, and certainly the first gulf between the values of parents and children that was given that name. Yet they also came to consciousness, and this was still true for those born in 1958 in Italy, before the so-called economic miracle had gathered speed to the extent of radically transforming the environment in which they and their parents were living.

Their grandparents will have been born towards the end of the nineteenth century. Their parents had grown up during the interwar years, which in Italy meant the totalitarian fascist state of Benito Mussolini. They were teenagers not in the swinging Sixties, but in the 'anni di piombo', the leaden and politically ossified years of the 1970s; and they experienced the Cold War not so much as a realization of the threat of nuclear destruction, but as a steady state in which nothing appeared likely to change. They experienced the Cold War as the normal. Not only were they able to glimpse in Italy, through their grandparental generations, an almost pre-industrial world, but they were surrounded by signs not merely of the fascist decades, but also of two world wars, and, in Italy, a brutal and highly politicized civil war as well.

Yet the dates given for the poems in Pietro De Marchi's first collection, 1990–1999, suggest a further irony, for it would seem that the poet only began completing work he was willing to collect *after* the fall of the Berlin Wall in 1989, and in the year of the fall of the Soviet Union. That's to say, he emerges as a poet at the very moment that the ideological, cultural and political framework of the post-war 'settlement' was undergoing a transformative change, ushering in the much more confused and confusing states of affairs that we are now obliged to imagine as the normal. One of the first signs of this change to be felt in Italy was a strong sensation during the 1990s that as the world was changing so, at the same time, historical memory appeared to be suffering a strange bout of amnesia. It is the consciousness of such a strategic, tactical and accidental forgetting for those in this particularly betwixt-and-between generation that goes some way to explaining the repertory of impulses and motivations shaping the poems presented and translated here.

Drawing attention to aesthetic allegiances through epigraphs and dedications is already a way of remembering things, but in De Marchi's case those very allegiances speak to the generational gaps and intermittences sketched above. The *Linea Lombarda* was the name given to a 1952 anthology of poetry edited by Luciano Anceschi. It included at least two poets, Luciano Erba and Giorgio Orelli, from whom De Marchi has learned much and to whom he as written tributes – the latter of these having written the preface to his first collection, *Parabole smorzate* (1999). Here's how I attempted to characterize the Lombard Line in the introduction to Erba's *The Greener Meadow: Selected Poems* (2006):

> Anceschi identified and presented a grouping of poets based in or around Milan with roots in the Luino-Como-Varese 'Lake District' of northern Italy. He saw them as sharing a poetry of objects, of understatement, irony, and self-criticism, which included social commentary and cultural commitment – but only if mediated through a sceptical grid of humanistic intelligence and aesthetic detachment.

However grateful for the attention the anthologized poets might have been (Roberto Rebora, Giorgio Orelli, Nelo Risi, Renzo Modesti, Luciano Erba) and how happy to have been grouped as exemplifying 'la poesia dell'oggetto', their independent heterogeneity and quietly pointed irony, qualities that De Marchi has adapted for his own themes, is exemplified in Erba's short later poem which takes the 'Linea' of this title to be a railway line, and situates himself as if between two Milanese stations:

LOMBARD LINE

Prejudices, commonplaces I adore
I like to think that there are
always girls with clogs in Holland
that they play the mandolin at Naples
that just a bit anxious you await me
when I change between Lambrate and Garibaldi.

Erba is doubtless right that literary genealogies are inclined to encapsulate prejudice and commonplace, and Vittorio Sereni, a definitively emblematic poet of Milan and the Italian lakes, ruled himself out of his friend's anthology for such reasons; but the extent and amorphousness of this grouping can be sensed from its Italian Wikipedia entry, one which divides the *Linea Lombarda* into four generations, with the poets from Anceschi's anthology drawn from the third and fourth, and it places at its head none other than Alessandro Manzoni, born in 1785. Thus in talking of this line or tradition we might be referring to a strand in mid-twentieth-century Italian poetry, or a cultural ambience, what the Wikipedia entry calls 'a typically Lombard *Weltanschauung*'.

Identifying the roots of the former, that strand in modern and contemporary Italian poetry, does, though, connect it with the continuance and evolution of a major vein in the corpus. Sereni, remembering Giuseppe Ungaretti at the time of his death in 1970, not only called himself the older poet's 'son' but quoted some of the last words Ungaretti said to him about preferring Milan to Rome; and Sereni expresses his initial surprise at this, only to recall the early poems from *Allegria* set in the city, lines which, he says, 'drew me, as a youth, to his poetry'. Again we find ourselves on the city's transport system, but this time on an evening tram:

Even tonight will pass

This loneliness going around
shadow of the tram-wires rocking
on the damp tarmac

I'm watching the heads of tram drivers
half-asleep
nodding off

This brief imagistic urban poetry that wrings the neck of eloquence with its lightly unrhymed free-verse has had its influence on almost everyone, but especially on poets who know what the trams look like and have walked over that 'damp tarmac' or under the 'tram-wires rocking'. The earliest section of Ungaretti's first collection, where this poem appears, also contains pieces set in the Paris of Apollinaire's Cubists, and this is the precise moment when the vanguard experiments in French poetry and painting make their way across the Alps, continuing a strain of Francophile influence deriving from the exploits of Napoleon at the Bridge of Lodi in 1796 and recreated in Stendhal's Milan at the opening of *The Charterhouse of Parma*. This Francophile thread in Milanese poetry can also be traced in De Marchi's numerous pieces set in Paris or along the Seine.

In his early 'Garden Concert', Sereni may be holidaying in Luino, but his thoughts are inflected not only by Mussolini's war in Abyssinia, but also, thanks to Luino's frontier railway station, that moment across the entire continent:

> At this hour
> they're watering gardens all over Europe.
> Hoarse trumpet of spray
> gathers warlike children,
> echoes in sounds of water
> far as this bench's shade.

Thus, in that first stanza, that specifically Lombard *Weltanschauung* turns out to be unusually European and in that might only reflect the changing fortunes of Milan and environs before unification, a city governed at one time or another by the Spanish Bourbons, the Austro-Hungarian Empire, and both Revolutionary and Imperial France. Just so, in 'Qualtieri solari', Erba can announce that 'it seemed to me I was in Europe' or in another poem about his home town that calls it by its German name, 'Mailand', he concludes by alluding to the Germanic loan-words for doughnuts and pastries, and confessing:

> truth was going home myself I'd be wearing
> a heavy odour of *krapfen* and *kipfeln*
> red cushions and yellow-black trams
> I'd be climbing stairs without elevator
> of ordinary people, of ordinary Europe

Erba's poetry is a preeminent example of how to address the crisis of subject matter, in which writing about yourself is selfishly egoistical and writing about others is appropriative. He addressed the final frontier of *terra incognita* in Italian poetry by concentrating on the lineaments of private and family life. The family is of great importance in Italy, of course, and it is perhaps unsurprising in this light that there should be a school of family therapy associated with Milan. Italian poetry has distinctly more poems in which men write poems on their mothers, as well as on their fathers, as is more frequent in Anglophone poetic contexts. The concretion, the objects, of the *Linea Lombarda* then find their natural focus in the minutiae of domestic situations – within which the understatement and self irony function to mediate complex feelings of attachment and dependence crossed with their opposites.

A second of Sereni's father figures, one pictured by the poet angrily going from one Milan square to another in the aftermath of the 1948 elections, was Umberto Saba (1883–1957), and in his work a different strand of lightness was wedded to a more formal verse, as in his 'Portrait of my Little Girl' from *Cose leggere e vaganti* (1920), whose title phrase derives from its final line:

> My little girl with a ball in her hand,
> with large eyes the colour of sky
> and her summer outfit: 'Daddy,'
> she tells me, 'I want to go out with you today.'
> And I was thinking: of the many apparitions
> admired in the world, I know very well
> to which I'd compare my little girl.
> Certainly to foam, to the seaside foam
> whitening waves, to that blue wake
> emerging from roofs and the wind disperses;
> likewise to the clouds, the indifferent clouds
> being made and unmade in clear sky
> and to other light and roaming things.

Saba's *Canzoniere* initiated the intimist and domestic thread in Italian poetry, too, with its many poems dedicated to feelings for his wife and daughter. In an essay on De Marchi's work reprinted as an afterword to *Der Schwan und die Schaukel / Il cigno e l'altalena* (2009), Fabio Pusterla notes the presence of Saba not only in a shared attachment to a lightness of touch, but also in the direct allusion to 'La capra' ('The Nanny-goat') in the sonnet 'At the Corner of Freiestrasse' where early in the last century Saba could refer to the goat's 'Semitic face' but, after all that has happened, De Marchi 'Non puoi dire: semita'. He can't use the word, although he is able to cite it in this negating form.

Urban isolation and fond feeling, a lightness of lyrical occasion and technique, a certain self-consciousness or self-mockery, and a commitment to embodying the lineaments of an occasion, often with political overtones, but without elaborating its significance too far beyond the moment itself – all of these features can be found too in 'The Black Trout' by Eugenio Montale, a tacitly ironic love poem set in Reading (England), to which De Marchi also alludes:

> Curved on the evening water
> graduates in Economics,
> Doctors of Divinity,
> the trout sniffs at and clears off,
> its carbuncular flash
> is a ringlet of yours undone
> in the bath, a sigh rising
> from your office catacombs.

But I have said that De Marchi is a poet from the Swiss branch of the Lombard Line, and to appreciate what this might mean we need to remember how close, for the lake poets of northern Italy, the border with Switzerland is, and how, to the north of the country, not only do you have the German-speaking Südtirol on the southern side of the border, but the Italian-speaking cantons of the Swiss Federation, of Ticino, over it to the north. This border is the literal frontier metaphorically extended, with the help of Conrad's *The Shadow Line* and Hemingway's *A Farewell to Arms*, in Sereni's first collection *Frontiera* (1941); and while its poet was a POW in North Africa between 1943 and 1945, his configuration of that border would be experienced as a site of real escape.

Just as Renzo, the hero of Manzoni's novel, had done in attempting to avoid capture after his misfortunes in Milan by passing into the Veneto in *I promessi sposi*, so would Franco Fortini and Luciano Erba, among many others, cross from the Republic of Salò into internment in Switzerland, a border crossing whose consequences figure in a number of their poems. Meanwhile, in the person of Giorgio Orelli (1921–2013), born in Canton Ticino, we have a Lombard Line mentor poet who was in fact Swiss, and whose collected poems De Marchi has edited for the Oscar series published by Mondadori. The first two stanzas from his early 'In the Family Circle' sketch a traditional context from which it may make no sense to flee but many would have to leave, figured by the returning dead:

> A funerary light, one quenched,
> re-freezes the conifers
> with their bark enduring beyond death,
> and all is still in this shell
> hollowed out tenderly by time:
> in the family circle
> from which it makes no sense to flee.

> Within a silence so well-known
> the dead are more alive than the living:
> from cleaned rooms smelling of camphor
> they come down by trap-doors in warm rooms
> replenished with wood, adjust their own portraits,
> revisit the stall to look once more
> at the brown, the pure-bred animals.

Orelli concludes: 'And me, to a more / discreet love of life I am restored...'. The senior poet characterized De Marchi's work as distinguished by its 'arguzia' (pointed wit) in his preface to *Parabole smorzate*. The multilingual, multi-cultural border territory of a Milanese poet who has lived since 1984 in Swiss-German-speaking Zurich is the landscape of Pietro De Marchi's poetry, and it makes him a poet intensely conscious of displacements, language differences, and how they mark a person as inescapably connected to or not belonging in a place, a place where Swiss or Swiss-based Italophone poetry is often published in bilingual editions with German translations *en face*.

Of course, the linguistic differences inevitably revealed in a translation can also be inspiring, and can help to put us back in touch with those who are dearest to us, as here in 'Disillusion and Meter', the first of De Marchi's poems I translated, challenged by the fact that because the metrics of English and Italian are quite distinct, both in how they work and how they are named, the final line of his sonnet would have to be transposed into differently self-referential terms if it were to make sense. The starting point for De Marchi's poem is his reading some words of Montale's from his late poem 'A tarda notte' (Late at Night) translated by Harry Thomas ('Now after many years the other voice / doesn't remember and maybe thinks I'm dead'):

> At Heathrow, in the airport,
> to trick away the wait
> I read a Montale in English translation,
> and back to mind comes the other summer
>
> when my father asked me on the phone
> if any post had arrived,
> but not stuff of no importance to him,
> electricity bills and bank statements.

> 'Postcards, for instance?'
> No, sorry, I was saying, there's nothing,
> and so he pronounced that phrase
>
> which now I repeat to myself without let-up
> ('You see they think that I'm already dead'),
> a perfect pentameter with second-foot caesura.

Here many of De Marchi's themes and affections characteristically coincide. There is: a tacit crossing of borders and language barriers in the Heathrow waiting area; an encounter with a familiar source of inspiration, but in the estranging form of an English translation; a *memento mori* in the form of a much-loved father's words, which may, or may not, be recalling the Nobel laureate's lines, words concerning a simple domestic incident; all these focused upon the role of the accuracy of poetic sound-sense structures in forming what Robert Frost famously called 'a stay against confusion'.

I have mentioned these Italian poets, and cited a few of my translations from them, to suggest the kinds of literary tradition from which De Marchi sets out, and to which his work has already begun to return. Making a large selection from his work available to an Anglophone readership is to suggest that his poetry deserves to find a home in that larger international heritage to which he has also dedicated himself in interview. To my mind, here is a poet who has recognized the challenges for a writer of his generation who finds himself in a globalising world of accelerated change and ever shortening memory span, of information overload and chronic lack of time to think and feel truly. His poetry exemplifies how a sensibility and a conscience can create authentic art out of such pressures and contradictions, offering spaces in which we are once more invited to both think and feel as truly as we are able.

NOTE ON THE TRANSLATIONS

As in my earlier books of translated poems, and as argued for in *Poetry & Translation: The Art of the Impossible* (2010), the aim here has been to combine fidelity to the original poems with a commitment to make poems and that work in English. The idea of fidelity in translation, as in other things in life, requires the acceptance and accommodation of differences. As I argue in that critical study of poetry translation practices, this art, which has been described as to all intents and purposes impossible (not least because the musics of languages are so irreproducibly different), is not ruled out because of those impossibilities but challenged to achieve what it can within those defining conditions – at whose heart is the acceptance of the irreducible incompatibilities of other languages and poetic traditions. It is after all not the easy similarities, but the intractable differences that prompt and inspire the translator of poetry to make such forays into 'the impossible'.

In his 2019 essay 'Translation and Tradition, and the Myth of Untranslatability', Pietro De Marchi reminds us of words by Luciano Erba in his Introduction to *Dei cristalli naturali e altri versi tradotti (1950–1990)*, where he described translation as 'above all a great recycling operation on materials supplied by the tradition' and De Marchi adds that whoever 'wants really to translate in a language cannot fail to take account of the tradition expressed in that language', underlining Erba's invitation 'not to refuse, rather to embrace', like an 'additional perfection', echoes, resonances, inlays or even thefts. 'We are', De Marchi continues, 'in that double game of losses and compensations about which Franco Fortini has spoken', explaining that –

> if the intertextual aura that encircles a text is almost inevitably lost in the target language, it can nonetheless be compensated for, at least in part, with the assistance of this target language's literary tradition. But the recourse to the tradition or more strictly to the literary culture tied to the language in which one translates is obviously welcomed even there where it is not, in the text to translate, a recognizable or declared hypertext.

De Marchi's essay was first published in a 2019 collection he edited with colleagues from the University of Zurich and called, bilingually, *Zwischen den Sprachen / Entre les langues* (Between the Languages). The import of his final point here appears to be that – thanks to the interrelations of languages, the histories of exchange and engrafting between them, and, equally, perhaps, the tendency of writers to be on the whole outward looking and inspired by elsewheres – that even where there is no obvious presence of the target language's literary culture in the original text, still, it is welcomed *in potentia* by means of the mutually recognizing and inter-defining co-existence of language cultures in the world.

Though I have never quite had the confidence to assert as much myself, until now, that is, in responding to the act of translating those words of De Marchi's into English, my own writings on this subject, gathered in *Poetry & Translation: The Art of the Impossible,* which includes a chapter on implications in Osip Mandelstam's nostalgia for a world culture, an idea first formulated in the word *Weltliteratur* by Goethe, I believe, are in full accord with this profession of De Marchi's, while the presentation of this selection of his poems does its best to live up to these principles. It does so by presenting the poem in an *en face* bilingual edition, so that the linguistic inspiration of the originals, their thematic, contextual, and linguistic bindings and structures, may be appreciated either alone, or in light of the solutions that these promptings have inspired in the English translations that face them.

When translating these poems, I have done my best, in light of those comments above by Erba and Fortini, both poets I was lucky enough to meet and have translated, simultaneously to attend to the poetic promptings of the second language and, as much as humanly possible, to cast the draft renderings of the originals into rhythmical units inevitably derived from experience of poetry in English; while, when revising, I have attempted to enhance the poetic qualities of the translation even when remaining faithful to as many aspects of the original as I was able. In this way I have hoped to produce a book that effectively represents the qualities of Pietro De Marchi's poetry for those that can appreciate the originals, for those that can make out the originals with the help of translations that cleave closely to the shape and structure of the work on the left hand pages, and for those whose sense of this poetry has to be grasped at the remove of my translations.

Note on the Translations　21

Even where I have chosen to render lines, words and phrases differently, I have benefitted greatly from the versions of De Marchi's work in Marco Sonzogni's translation for *Here and not Elsewhere: Selected Poems 1990–2010* (Toronto: Guernica Editions, 2012). I have also found assistance and confirmation for intuitions and English possibilities from the German versions by Christoph Ferber published in *Der Schwan und die Schaukel / Il cigno e l'altalena: Gedichte und Prosastücke 1990–2008* (Zurich: Limmat Verlag 2009) and in *Das Orangenpapier / La carta delle arance* (Zurich: Limmat Verlag, 2018).

Finally, I would like to thank the poet Pietro De Marchi for his friendship and support while working on this project, and his wife Antonella for her good will and hospitality. These translations would not have come about had I not encountered by chance a copy of *Das Orangenpapier / La carta delle arance* in a bookshop in Winterthur, Switzerland, in September 2018, for which opportunity I am indebted to the hospitality of my elder daughter Matilde and to Raphael Roten. My wife, Ornella Trevisan, has, as ever, been patience itself in helping with my efforts, and, last but by no means least, there has been the perpetual challenge of my younger daughter Giulia's perfect pitch and multilingual capacities to help me keep my feet on the ground – which is surely where a poet's ought to try and be, after all.

Peter Robinson
December 2021

DA

PARABOLE SMORZATE

(1999)

FROM

STUNNED PARABLES

(1999)

PARABOLE SMORZATE

Se l'avversario è più forte che mai
se con urlo strozzato si avventa sulla palla
e affonda di diritto
e incrocia col rovescio a due mani
tu non lo assecondare nel gioco a fondo campo
perché alla lunga ti sfiata ti spompa e alla fine
non avrai scampo un suo passante
ti infilerà

Tu invece rompi il suo ritmo
smorza la palla liftala dàlle
più effetto che puoi
fa' che ricada appena al di là della
rete.

from Parabole smorzate / Stunned Parables (1999)

STUNNED PARABLES

If the opponent's stronger than ever
if he attacks the ball with strangled cry
and buries a forehand
and responds with two-hand crosscourt
don't indulge him with a baseline game
because in the long run he'll wind deflate you
you'll not in the end escape his passing shot
it'll get you

Rather you break his rhythm
you stun the ball you lift it give it
such spin as you can
making it drop down just over
the net.

CAPRICCIO

Si fa di celluloide il mondo fuori,
voci doppiate, grida soffocate
dallo schermo di vetro...
È un istante, poi tutto

si appiattisce, ripiombi
nel sonno, nel *sueño*...
Il mondo si dilegua in verticale:
e allora gufi, pipistrelli,

un cane che è un gatto
e altri effetti speciali, prevalenza del nero.
Ma la mano che ti scuote, la voce

che ti chiama («Su dài, dobbiamo scendere»)
è la mano del mondo e la sua voce
vera.

from Parabole smorzate / Stunned Parables (1999)

CAPRICCIO

It's made of celluloid, the world outside,
dubbed voices, suffocated cries
from the glass screen…
A blink it is, then all

is flattened, you tumble
back into sleep, in the *sueño*…
The world's dispersed in vertical:
and then bats, owls,

a dog that's a cat
and other special effects, predominantly black.
But the hand that shakes you, the voice

calling you ('Come on now, we've got to get off')
is the world's hand and its own true
voice.

NON LONTANO DA DOVE

la guerra non è un gioco,
ragazzi coi fucili
giocano alla guerra.

Uno è più svelto a sparare, fa fuoco
con la bocca ed esulta trionfante:
«Adesso tu sei morto, cadi a terra!»

Ma l'altro non s'arrende. Dice che non vale.
Morire? Non gli va. Neanche per finta,
neanche per gioco.

from Parabole smorzate / Stunned Parables (1999)

NOT FAR FROM WHERE

war isn't a game
children with rifles
are playing at war.

Quicker on the trigger, one fires
with his mouth and triumphantly cries:
'You're dead now, fall on the ground!'

But the other won't surrender. Says it doesn't count.
Die? He won't. Not even pretending,
not even in play.

CON VALENTINA, DALLE ANATRE

I

L'hanno vista arrivare
col sacchetto di plastica
e a gara tutte insieme (tranne *Fritzli*)
le sono corse incontro sulla neve.
È la nonna delle anatre:
è lei che ha dato il nome a *Fritzli*,
l'anatra che zoppica.

II

Sì, zoppica, lo vedi anche da te:
bisogna che qualcuno se ne occupi.
Se vola non si nota,
e neppure se nuota,
ma ora sul laghetto
c'è una crosta di ghiaccio
e due dita di neve.

III

Ricordi, l'anno scorso,
quell'anatra che aveva il becco storto?
Spezzavi il pane in pezzi piccolissimi,
poi le andavi *vicino vicinissimo*,
vincendo la paura.

from Parabole smorzate / Stunned Parables (1999)

WITH VALENTINA, AT THE DUCKS

    I

They saw her approach
with the plastic bag
and competing all together (minus *Fritzli*)
they ran towards her on the snow.
She's the ducks' grandmother:
it's she who gave the name to *Fritzli*,
the duck that has a limp.

    II

Yes, he limps, you see it too:
someone needs to care for him.
If he's flying you don't notice,
and neither if he swims,
but on the small lake now
there's a crust of ice
and two fingers of snow.

    III

Remember, a year ago,
that duck who had a twisted beak?
You broke the bread into tiniest pieces,
then you went up *near, so very near*,
conquering your fear.

UNA PAGINA DI CIELO

«Scrivere ordinatamente una pagina
di cielo e una di cieco»
dal *Diario di seconda*, 1965–1966

Qui ci vorrebbe un pennello cinese.
I colori sarebbero il bianco del foglio
(questo cielo di ovatta)
ed il nero di china
(quel nero di nubi laggiù).

«Se oggi seren non è,
doman seren sarà.
Se non sarà seren,
si rasserenerà».

Forse è meglio aspettare.
Più sereni domani
scriveremo una pagina intera,
di un cielo non cieco,
con la più bella delle biro blu.

from Parabole smorzate / Stunned Parables (1999)

A PAGE OF SKY

'Neatly write a page of sky (*cielo*)
and one of blind (*cieco*)'
from the *Year Two Workbook*, 1965–1966

Here we'd need a Chinese brush.
Colours would be the page's white
(this sky of cotton wool)
and the China black
(that black of clouds down there).

'If it's not fine today,
it may be tomorrow.
If it don't turn out fine,
it'll clear you know.'

Perhaps we'd better wait.
If tomorrow is finer
we'll write one page complete,
of a sky not blind,
with the most beautiful of blue biros.

IMMAGINATE UNA COPPIA...

Immaginate una coppia di anziani ciclisti,
lui che è in testa a dettare l'andatura
e ogni tanto si volta a controllare
compreso del suo ruolo d'apripista,

lei che è a ruota e pedala concentrata, le mani
ben strette sul manubrio.
Ed ora immaginate lei che a un tratto
si rialza sulla sella, esita un attimo,

stacca una mano, l'altra, dal manubrio e prova,
come fosse la prima volta prova
ad andare senza mani.

Immaginate, immaginate, intanto
io li vedo qui davanti
pedalare come in gara contro il tempo.

from Parabole smorzate / Stunned Parables (1999)

IMAGINE A COUPLE...

Imagine a couple of antique cyclists,
him in front dictating the pace
now and then turning to check
his frontrunner role understood,

her at his wheel pedaling intently, hands
good and tight on the handlebars.
And now imagine her all of a sudden
sit up on the saddle, hesitate a moment,

a hand off, the other, from the bars now she tries,
as if it were her first attempt
to go on with no hands.

Imagine, imagine, meanwhile
I see them up ahead here
pedal as if they're competing in a time trial.

RETTILI

Se solo potessero
farebbero sogni di un lusso
sfrenato, avere due code
o vivere a Capri,

o sogni concreti, da mordere,
da masticare,
una formica, una vespa stecchita,
un'ala di cicala,

o anche sogni più tetri,
un'ombra sul sasso,
un fischio nell'aria, poi il senso
di qualcosa che manca.

Ma i rettili non sognano.
È questione di sangue: freddo.

from Parabole smorzate / Stunned Parables (1999)

REPTILES

If only they could
they would have dreams
of unbridled luxury, have
two tails or live at Capri,

or material dreams, of biting,
of chewing an ant,
a dropped-dead wasp,
a cicada's wing,

or even grimmer dreams,
a shadow on the stone,
a whistle in the air, then the sense
there's something missing.

But reptiles don't dream.
It's a question of their blood: cold.

FOTO DI PAESAGGIO CON FIGURE

Il paesaggio, per me, può stare sullo sfondo.
Qui a Bergen, per esempio,
lo spettacolo è il mare con le dune,
non c'è niente da dire...

Eppure mi distraggo e guardo i passeri,
una dozzina almeno attavolati
due tavoli più in là, fanno lo slalom
fra tazze, cucchiaini e briciole di toast.

Di tanto in tanto guardo anche la donna
che è al tavolo dei passeri e non bada
ai passeri e agli sguardi e guarda il mare.

Per discrezione metto a fuoco i passeri,
ma inquadro anche la donna
e dietro a lei le dune e dietro il mare.

from Parabole smorzate / Stunned Parables (1999)

LANDSCAPE PHOTO WITH FIGURES

The landscape, for me, can stay in the background.
Here at Bergen, for example,
the performance is the sea with dunes,
there's not a thing to say…

Still it's distracting and I look at the sparrows
coming in to land, a dozen at least,
two tables further, they do the slalom
between cups, teaspoons, and crumbs of toast.

From time to time I look too at the woman
at the table with the sparrows who takes no notice
of the sparrows and looks and looks at the sea.

I focus from discretion on the sparrows,
but frame the woman too
and behind her the dunes and behind them the sea.

VERSO MARINA

Rischia grosso il ramarro maremmano
se sotto la gran fersa dell'estate
attraversa la pista
ciclabile e non vede
la ruota che si arresta,
e non legge il cartello che ripete
per l'ennesima volta la minaccia:
PROBABILE CADUTA RAMI E PIGNE.

Io, ciclista alfabeta,
mi affido al dio del caso, se mi assiste,
sfido l'azzardo di una
pineta minata dall'alto,
sotto una pioggia di aghi
riparto, riprendo il mio ritmo
pronto allo scarto,
al rapido zig zag
o alla frenata brusca
per ramarri che cambiano siepe,
per rami o pigne in libera
caduta.

from Parabole smorzate / Stunned Parables (1999)

TOWARDS MARINA

He risks a lot, the Maremman lizard
if under the great heat of summer
he crosses the bike route
and does not see
the stopping wheel,
and doesn't read the sign
repeating its warning ad infinitum:
FALLING BRANCHES AND PINECONES LIKELY.

Me, a literate cyclist,
I trust to the god of chance, if he'll help me,
braving the risk
of a pine forest mined from above,
under a raining of needles,
I set off once more, take up my rhythm
ready for the swerve,
the rapid zigzag
or hasty braking
for lizards changing hedgerow,
for branches or pinecones
in free fall.

LISBONA, RUA GARRETT

A Brasileira è su tutte le guide
e quindi tutti ci vanno.
La statua del poeta li aspetta
per la foto di rito.
C'è chi gli siede accanto, sulla sedia di bronzo,
chi gli monta sulle gambe accavallate
accavallando le gambe,
chi gli sfiora le mani, la tesa del cappello,
chi gli getta le braccia intorno al collo.
C'è infine anche chi non si ferma,
ma passando gli dà
tre pacche sulla spalla.

Il giorno dopo in aereo leggo che in Brasile
un tascabile costa un sesto del minimo mensile.

from Parabole smorzate / Stunned Parables (1999)

LISBON, RUA GARRETT

A Brasileira's in all of the guidebooks
and so everybody goes there.
The poet's statue awaits them
for the ritual photo.
There are those sit beside him, on the bronze seat,
those who climb on his crossed legs
crossing their own legs,
those who touch his hands, the brim of his hat,
who throw an arm about his neck.
There's even one finally who does not stop,
but going by gives him
three pats on the back.

I read on my flight the next day
how a paperback book in Brazil
costs a sixth of the minimum monthly pay.

ALL'ANGOLO DI FREIESTRASSE

Basta poco, un cappello nero, un nero cappotto
(niente di strano a queste latitudini),
e un uomo studia il passo, ti raggiunge
e d'un fiato *Raphèl maí amècche* comincia a dire…

Tu non capisci, non rispondi, lo deludi
e un dubbio allora lo punge
che quasi già un dubbio non è,
cambia lingua, domanda: *Sind Sie Jude?*

In quell'istante, sul suo viso perplesso
(non puoi dire: semita),
leggi l'ansia di un uomo in fuga da tutta la vita.

Tu pensi: il tempo passa,
la storia si ripete o lascia strascichi.
Lui già saluta e imbocca Freiestrasse.

from Parabole smorzate / Stunned Parables (1999)

AT THE CORNER OF FREIESTRASSE

Little will do, a black hat, a black coat
(not at all odd at these latitudes),
and a man speeds his pace, he joins you
and *Raphèl maí amècche* with a gasp begins to say...

You don't understand, don't reply, you dismay
him, and then a doubt pricks him
which is almost already not a doubt,
he changes language, asks: *Sind Sie Jude?*

In that instant, on his face, perplexed,
(you can't say: Semitic),
you read the angst of a man in lifelong flight.

You think: time passes,
history repeats itself or leaves traces.
Already he's waving and heads down Freiestrasse.

FRONTESPIZIO

'Livros são papéis pintados com tinta.'
       Fernando Pessoa

Ma chi lo dice
che la carta è felice
quando annusa nell'aria questo odore
di inchiostro? Sarà vero
che la titilla il solletico
delle mie dita?
Chi ci assicura che non ha paura
di una matita ben appuntita?
Chi lo sa cosa prova
quando una penna la sfiora,
magari si dispera
nel vedersi allo specchio
gli scarabocchi, gli sgorbi, le macchie.
Non ha poi grandi pretese,
la carta, come tutti
vuole arrivare alla fine del mese.
Forse il suo sogno sarebbe di vivere
in santa pace così come è nata,
bianca immacolata,
per poi sparire
non appena incomincia ad ingiallire.

from Parabole smorzate / Stunned Parables (1999)

FRONTISPIECE

'Books are papers painted with ink.'
                Fernando Pessoa

But who is to say
that the paper's gay
when on the air it sniffs this smell
of ink? Will it be true
that it thrills to the touch
of my fingers?
Who'll assure us that it's not afraid
of a freshly sharpened pencil?
Who knows what it feels
when a pen touches it,
maybe it despairs
on seeing in the mirror
the scribbles, scrawls, the stains.
It doesn't have high hopes,
paper, just like everyone
it wants to get to the end of the month.
Perhaps its dream would be to live
in perfect peace as it was born,
immaculately white,
to vanish then
no sooner does it start to yellow.

IL CIGNO E L'ALTALENA

È fermo eppure dondola
il cigno che lento si liscia
sull'acqua di raso del lago:
lo sospinge una bava

di vento, lo raggiunge
impercettibile l'onda.
Transita al largo un kayak,
i soliti passeri a riva

saltellano, perlustrano la ghiaia.
L'alternativo con cane si allena
a lanciare in aria il bastone

per riprenderlo al volo.
Intanto tu vai dallo scivolo
all'altalena.

from Parabole smorzate / Stunned Parables (1999)

THE SWAN AND THE SWING

It's stopped yet still rocks
the swan slowly gliding
on the lake's smooth water:
a filament of wind

impels it, imperceptibly
it's reached by the wave.
The lake's crossed by a kayak,
upon the shore the usual

sparrows hop, they comb the gravel.
The hipster with a dog
flings a stick in the air,

trains him to catch it in flight.
In the meantime you go
to the swing from the slide.

GABBIANI E FOLAGHE

Non appena la Frau
vestita di blau
getta dal ponte
vicino alla Migros
un sacco e una sporta
di pane e di briciole

non sono le folaghe,
le sue beniamine,
sono i gabbiani
che beccano il pane.

Gabbiani e folaghe
non vanno d'accordo
neppure a pagarli,
nemmeno a Zurigo.
Ma non lo sa, la Frau
vestita di blau?

from Parabole smorzate / Stunned Parables (1999)

SEAGULLS AND COOTS

No sooner does the Frau
all dressed in *blau*
throw from the bridge
near to the Migros
a bag and a basket
of bread and breadcrumbs

than it isn't the coots,
her favourites,
it's the seagulls
that peck at the bread.

Seagulls and coots,
they don't get along,
not even if paid to,
not even in Zurich.
But doesn't she know that, the Frau
all dressed in *blau*?

PROMESSE DA MARINAIO

I bevitori di birra in Irlanda,
se talvolta si pentono,
non è per sempre,
ma solo fino alla prossima pinta.

Valgono, i loro pentimenti,
come i propositi di Zeno, U. S.
(ultima sigaretta!), o come le promesse
dei marinai.

E visto che si parla delle loro promesse,
era una scena da ex voto
quella che mi immaginai:
la tempesta, la nave, i marinai

in ginocchio che invocano la Vergine
apparsa tra le nuvole e le promettono,
se scampano alla morte,
di andare a messa e non peccare più.

Questo – mi aveva spiegato la nonna,
piissima donna –
voleva dire promessa da marinaio,
questo e nient'altro.

A chi davvero facessero promesse
da marinaio i marinai
lo imparai molto, ma molto più tardi,
e tuttavia meglio tardi che mai.

from Parabole smorzate / Stunned Parables (1999)

PROMISES FROM SAILORS

Beer drinkers in Ireland
if now and then they do repent,
it's not for ever,
but only until the next pint.

They count, their repentances,
like Zeno's intentions, L. C.
(last cigarette!), or like the promises
of sailors.

And speaking of their promises,
there was that ex-voto scene,
the one I would imagine:
storm, ship, the sailors

kneeling, evoking the Virgin
revealed through clouds and promising,
if spared from death
to attend mass and to sin no more.

This – my grandma would explain,
most pious woman –
is what promises from sailors meant,
this and nothing else.

To those who would truly make
promises from sailors, sailors
have taught me much, but much later,
and anyway better late than never.

RIME BACIATE

Le scrissi delle rime
in forma di enigma:
lei era l'anguicrinita
Gorgone, io il languido
amante pietrificato
dal suo sguardo.

Mi rispose per le rime:
io ero la Sfinge, lei Edipo?
I conti non tornavano.

Allora baciai le sue rime
come un amante romantico:
io non fui più di pietra,
lei non fu più di sasso.

from Parabole smorzate / Stunned Parables (1999)

KISSING RHYMES

I wrote the rhymes
in enigmatic form:
you were snake-haired
Gorgon, me languid
lover turned to stone
by your gaze.

You replied with the rhymes:
I was the Sphinx, you Oedipus?
The books didn't balance.

Then I made your rhymes kiss
as romantic lovers do:
me no longer petrified,
you no more stone too.

POESIA D'AMORE

A una lettura di poesia una donna vistosa anzi che no
(«È una cantante folk», mi sussurra il vicino), si alza
dal fondo della sala, domanda al poeta se non ha
mai scritto un libro tutto di poesie d'amore.

«Perché sa,
studiavo ai tempi nella scuola dove
insegnava Lei, saranno vent'anni e passa e Lei passava,
fra di noi ragazze, per uno a cui le donne piacciono».

Sorride lui, e intanto sbircia la moglie
seduta in prima fila con la figlia: «No, no,
non ho mai scritto un canzoniere in senso stretto,
ma vede, la poesia è quasi sempre poesia d'amore.

Voi piuttosto, perché non mi avete mai messo un fiore
sul manubrio della bici?
Erano cose così che mi aspettavo»,
dice, e sbircia di nuovo
la moglie che sorride con la figlia.

from Parabole smorzate / Stunned Parables (1999)

LOVE POETRY

At a poetry reading a rather loud woman
('She's a folksinger,' whispered my neighbour),
she rises from the back of the room, asks the poet
has he ever done a whole book of love poetry.

'Because you know,
I attended in my school days where you
taught, some twenty years past and you passed
amongst us girls, for the sort women like.'

Him, he smiles, and peers at his wife meanwhile
sitting in the front row with their daughter: 'No, no,
I've never, in the strict sense, written a love-song cycle,
but, you see, poetry's almost always love poetry.

You lot, though, why didn't you ever place a flower
on my bicycle handlebars?
That's just the sort of thing I expected,'
he says, and peers once more
at his wife, she smiling with their daughter.

SPIAGGIA LIBERA

La puoi credere viva
se ancora la rivolge la risacca,
ma se un'onda più lunga
la sputa capovolta
è una medusa morta
sulla riva.
      La gente
in tuta che smaltisce
ciccia e stress getta occhiate
distratte, non ha tempo per meduse,
morto o vive.

from Parabole smorzate / Stunned Parables (1999)

FREE BEACH

You can believe it's alive
if the undertow still turns it,
but if a longer wave
spits it out head-over-heels
it's a jellyfish dead
on the shore.
               The people
in sweatpants who burn off
fat and stress cast careless
glances, they've no time for jellyfish,
dead or alive.

da

REPLICA

(2006)

from

REPLY

(2006)

INGANNO OTTICO

Se l'aquilastro o falco pescatore
naturalmente fa quel che l'istinto gli detta e librandosi alto
si lascia trasportare dal vento, poi plana roteando
e sceso a pelo d'acqua per un attimo increspa
la superficie del lago, a pesca di coregoni o di persici,
provando e riprovando finché la fortuna l'assista nel becco;
se qualcuno ti presta il binocolo
e mentre guardi ti pare ad un tratto che il falco
con le larghe ali tese si schianti
contro i balconi balaustrati della riva opposta,
quasi subito sai che si tratta di un banale inganno ottico,
di un effetto di schiacciamento della prospettiva,
perché in realtà quel che conta e ti attrae
accade in mezzo al lago, non ha niente da spartire
con le dimore patrizie, il ghiaietto dei viali, i motoscafi
d'alto bordo ormeggiati nei garage.

from Replica / Reply (2006)

TROMPE L'ŒIL

If the osprey or the fish-hawk
does what instinct tells it naturally and hovering high
lets itself be carried on the wind, then circling glides
and dropped water-skimming for an instant ruffles
the lake surface, to catch white fish or perch,
trying and trying till luck assists it into the beak;
if somebody lends you binoculars
and while you look it seems suddenly the hawk
with broad wings stretched
crashes into the far shore's balustraded balconies,
you quickly see it's a banal trompe l'œil,
a flattened perspective effect,
because what really matters and draws you
takes place in the middle of the lake, has nothing to do
with patrician dwellings, avenues' fine gravel,
the high-end speedboats moored in their garages.

UNA SOVRAPPOSIZIONE PER GIAMPIERO NERI

Grande quanto un gufo reale
la civetta delle nevi (*Nyctea scandiaca*)
ruotava il capo arruffando le penne.
Ma non vedeva niente,
neanche un topo in fuga.
Non c'era niente,
tranne il bianco perenne.

from Replica / Reply (2006)

AN OVERLAY FOR GIAMPIERO NERI

Large as an eagle owl
the snowy one (*Nyctea scandiaca*)
twisted its head round ruffling its feathers.
But it didn't see a thing,
not so much as a mouse in flight.
No, there was nothing,
except the perpetual white.

LETTERA DA BINZ

a Fabio Pusterla

Dalle parti del maneggio
dove c'è quella pista d'atletica senza reti né cancelli
dove il tartan è d'un rosso così rosso
che pensi a un'anguria matura
dove l'erba del prato è d'un verde così verde
che non osi calpestarla
è lì che sosto, tutti i mercoledì,
nell'ora che mia figlia va a cavallo.
Ma l'altra settimana
lì c'erano i ragazzi delle scuole: s'allenavano,
saltavano, correvano nel sole.
Oggi invece la pista era in mano ai soldati,
tutti armati, non tutti fino ai denti:
qualcuno s'aggirava nei dintorni
misurando, fissando a terra pioli, cavi del telefono;
ai piedi di un castagno altri parlavano
a un compagno nascosto tra le foglie;
appaiati, due caccia
sfrecciavano nel cielo, verso est,
poi tornavano indietro col frastuono consueto.
S'avvertiva un disagio, un principio di paura.
Forse per questo un soldato passando mi ha detto: *Grüezi*.

Quando fu tempo di tornare al maneggio
lungo la strada ho raccolto una pera caduta: la parte
non marcia era d'un dolce
troppo dolce da dire.

from Replica / Reply (2006)

LETTER FROM BINZ

to Fabio Pusterla

From the equestrian centre
where there's that running track without gates or fences
where the surface is a red so red
you think of a ripe watermelon
where the meadow grass is a green so green
you don't dare tread on it
it's there every Wednesday I remain
for the hour my daughter goes horse-riding.
But the other week
there were school-kids: training,
jumping, running in the sun.
Today, though, the track's in the hands of soldiers,
all armed, though not all to the teeth:
someone was going about in the surroundings
measuring, pegging out the ground for telephone wires;
at a chestnut's foot others were talking
to a companion hidden in the leaves;
side by side, two fighters
arrowed through the sky, towards east,
then turned back with the usual racket.
It started unease, an inception of fear.
Maybe that's why a passing soldier said: *Good day.*

When it was time to return to the centre
on the road I picked up a fallen pear: the part
not rotten had a sweetness
much too sweet to say.

DAVANTI ALLA PINACOTECA

> '...how it takes place
> While someone else is eating...'
>   W. H. Auden, 'Musée des Beaux Arts'

Seduto a un tavolo del bar all'angolo
tra Brera e Fiori Chiari,
guardi e ascolti la vita quotidiana.
C'è chi racconta storie sue o d'altri,
storie di figli, di mariti e mogli.
C'è chi si fa spiegare la divina proporzione
perché ha l'esame questo pomeriggio
e ancora non la sa.
Quando passa un ragazzo un po' artista nel vestire,
si volta una ragazza e dice cazzo!, me ne sono innamorata.
In quel momento suona il cellulare: è sua madre,
l'hanno detto alla radio.
C'è chi da un altro tavolo s'informa:
sì, a Londra, stamattina, delle bombe nel metrò.
C'è chi arriva solo ora e non sa niente,
si siede, dà un'occhiata alla carta, poi ordina
vino bianco e prosciutto col melone.

from Replica / Reply (2006)

IN FRONT OF THE ART MUSEUM

'…how it takes place
While someone else is eating…'
        W. H. Auden, 'Musée des Beaux Arts'

Sat at a table in the corner bar
between Brera and Fiori Chiari
you watch and listen to the daily life.
There's those who tell their own and others' stories,
stories of children, of husbands and wives.
There's those who explain the Golden Section
because they have an exam this afternoon
and still they don't get it.
When a boy goes by dressed a bit like an artist,
a girl turns and says, shit!, I'm falling in love.
Her mobile goes off at that moment: it's her mother,
she's heard it on the radio.
There's those at another table who are informed:
yes, bombs, this morning, on the London Underground.
There's those who arrive only now and know nothing,
they settle down, glance at the menu, order then
white wine, melon and Parma ham.

ANNI SETTANTA

'Qui la storia del Carmagnola comincia
ad essere legata con quella del suo tempo.'
       Alessandro Manzoni

Fu sotto i portici dell'Arengario
che la sua storia cominciò a legarsi
con quella del suo tempo.
Ne uscì manganellato, l'occhio nero,
quattro punti, un grave stato
confusionale. All'ospedale
il commissario chiese
se era dei rossi o dei neri, poi disse:
la politica, sa, l'è roba sporca.
Come fare a spiegargli che passava
di lì per caso, andava in piazza Diaz
per via di una ricerca,
aveva quindici anni,
era al ginnasio…

from Parabole smorzate / Stunned Parables (1999)

THE SEVENTIES

'Here Carmagnola's story begins
to be attached to that of his time.'
      Alessandro Manzoni

It was under the Arengario's porticos
that his story began
to be attached to that of his time.
He came out beaten up, with a black eye,
four stitches, in a bad state
of concussion. At the hospital
the inspector asked him
if he was a red or a black, then said:
politics, you know, it's a dirty business.
How make him understand
he was there by chance, crossing Piazza Diaz
to do some research,
he was fifteen-years-old,
was in senior school…

ATTRAVERSANDO LA POLONIA

'...rosseggiavano lontani i campanili di Cracovia'
                Primo Levi, *La tregua*

Pecore, capre, cavalli.
Un uomo che munge una vacca in mezzo a un prato.
Bambini che corrono per guardare il treno che passa.
Ci si ferma in una stazione.
Non c'è quasi il tempo di accorgersi che siamo a O.
Case, antenne paraboliche, come altrove.
Si riparte.
Riprendo la lettura del mio libro.
Nie rozumiem po polsku.
Non capisco il polacco.

from Replica / Reply (2006)

CROSSING POLAND

'...far off the bell towers of Cracow were reddening.'
Primo Levi, *The Truce*

Sheep, goats, horses.
In the middle of a field a man's milking a cow.
Children who run to watch the passing trains.
We stop at a station.
There's hardly time to realize it's O.
Houses, satellite dishes, as elsewhere.
We set off again.
I return to my book-reading.
Nie rozumiem po polsku.
Polish I don't know.

PROMEMORIA DA UN LUOGO DI BETULLE
per Katia

Ogni volta che corri alla finestra
per distrarre la mente dalla vista
di quello che rimane dei sommersi,
lì fuori trovi sempre una betulla,

il prato, i fiori gialli, il cielo terso.
Potessimo bandire il nostro tempo,
tornare indietro a inizio Novecento,
qui avremmo solo un bosco di betulle,

le strade, qualche casa, la tranquilla
estate dei paesi di pianura.
Ma niente più cancella quei capelli

tosati, quegli occhiali di metallo,
quelle povere scarpe color polvere:
quello che non fu cenere, né fumo.

from Replica / Reply (2006)

MEMO FROM A PLACE OF BIRCHES
for Katia

Every time you run to the window
to distract your mind from the sight
of what remains of the smothered,
outside, you always find a birch,

the meadow, yellow flowers, wiped sky.
Could we banish our own time,
return to the early nineteen-hundreds,
here we'd have only a birch wood,

the roads, some houses, the tranquil
summer of the hamlets on the plain.
But nothing more deletes that hair

shaved off, those spectacles of metal,
those poor dust-coloured shoes:
what was neither ashes, nor smoke.

FUNERALE A BAAR

'quando fra un treno e l'altro un colombo si posa
sulle rotaie'
      Giorgio Orelli, 'In ripa di Tesino'

Mentre in chiesa il pastore legge e spiega
la prima delle Lettere ai Corinzi
con quello *speculum* e quell'*aenigmate*
e il conoscere e l'esser conosciuti,

come impone l'orario, puntuali
fuori passano i treni, poi ripassano
non lontani dal prato suburbano
dove il compianto già riposa in pace.

Parenti e amici ascoltano compunti
il *nunc* e il *tunc*, il *facie ad faciem*,
solo una donna è scossa da un singulto.

Ma nessuno là fuori sa arrestare
il regolare transito dei treni,
quel rumore di ruote, di rotaie.

FUNERAL AT BAAR

'when between one train and the next a dove settles
onto the rails'
        Giorgio Orelli, 'On the Ticino's Shore'

While in church the pastor reads and explains
the first of the Letters to the Corinthians
with that *speculum* and that *aenigmate*
and the knowing and the being known,

as the timetable requires, outside
trains pass on the dot, then pass again
not distant from the suburban meadow
where the mourned one already rests in peace.

Family and friends contritely listen
to the *nunc* and *tunc*, the *facie ad faciem*,
only one woman's shaken by a sob.

But nobody outside knows how to stop
the regular passing of the trains,
that rumble of wheels, of tracks.

QUI E NON ALTROVE

Che importa a questo punto
che in fondo al corridoio una finestra
inquadri tutto quanto il Resegone
e non come talvolta un disadorno
cortile d'ospedale? Eppure ha un senso
vederti proprio qui e non altrove, pensare
che il tuo viaggio, se termina, è qui,
accanto a questo grande
dipinto naturale.

from Replica / Reply (2006)

HERE AND NOT ELSEWHERE

What does it matter if at this point
at the end of a corridor a window
frames the entire Resegone
and not as so often a bare
hospital courtyard? Even if it makes sense
to see you truly here and not elsewhere,
to think that your journey if it ends, it ends here,
before this vast
natural canvas.

VARIAZIONI SU UN TEMA ANTICO

Dove saranno a quest'ora Vilmante,
la bella lituana, e Arneta e le altre?
E la più dolce di tutte, Ljudmila ucraina,

che un giorno di settembre, a Berlino,
chiedendole io se il marito,
di cui parlava spesso all'imperfetto,

sarebbe presto venuto a trovarla,
con un filo di voce mi disse
«*Mein Mann ... ist ... vermisst*»?

«Quel giorno uscì di case e poi nessuno,
più nessuno da allora l'ha visto.
Sono quattordici mesi che aspetto

notizie, che aspettiamo, io e Klarina,
ma lei è così piccola, non credo
che potrà ricordare».

Dove saranno a quest'ora Vilmante,
la bella lituana, e Arneta e le altre?
Ljudmila, dovunque tu sia,

perdona se ti ho messa in poesia.

from Replica / Reply (2006)

VARIATIONS ON AN OLD THEME

Where are they now, the lovely Lithuanian
Vilmante, and Arneta and the others?
And sweetest of all, Ukrainian Ljudmila

who, in Berlin, one September day,
when I asked her if the husband
she often spoke of in the imperfect

would soon be coming to find her,
in a whisper of a voice she told me
'*My husband ... is ... missing*'?

'That day he left the house and from then,
no one, nobody has seen him since.
It's been fourteen months I've waited

for news, we've waited, me and Klarina,
but she is so little I don't believe
she'll be able to remember.'

Where are they now, the lovely Lithuanian
Vilmante, and Arneta and the others?
Ljudmila, wherever you may be,

forgive me if I've put you into poetry.

DIARIO D'IRLANDA

I

Farida, la ragazza sudanese
che non smette di ridere e protrae così la notte
rimandando a domani la iattura
dei compiti d'inglese,
ci chiede se crediamo nel malocchio,
poi si fa seria e spiega che da loro, a Khartum, le discariche
sono abitate dai genii, dagli spiriti:
«È meglio che tu preghi, se mai ci passi accanto;
temono solo l'acqua calda, i demoni,
e non è sempre detto che tu l'abbia
a portata di mano».
Di certo Farida non sa nulla
della feniletilamina di cui leggo
in questo libro sulla storia del cacao:
ce n'è nel cioccolato, vi si dice,
e ha benefici influssi sull'umore;
la sostanza è la stessa che il cervello
rilascia in varie dosi
quando ti adiri o quando ti innamori.
E se non lo sa Farida,
potrà saperlo la gazza che atterra
sul prato del cortile e se ne infischia del vento
che fa l'Irlanda più sola,
più isola?

II

Bayside è tranquilla stasera. Non piove più, qualcuno
porta a passeggio il cane, le cellule fotoelettriche
l'abbagliano nel punto che passa vicino alla porta qui accanto.
Dal lungomare stasera vedresti tutto il golfo, e Sandycove

from Replica / Reply (2006)

IRELAND DIARY

I

Farida, the Sudanese girl
who won't stop laughing and so extends the night
putting off until tomorrow her
English homework curse,
she asks do we believe in the evil eye
then gets serious and explains how with them, in Khartoum,
the rubbish is lived in by genies, by spirits:
'It's better to pray, if you pass nearby them;
the demons, they're only afraid of hot water,
and it's not at all certain you'll always
have any to hand.'
Certainly Farida knows nothing
of the phenylethylamine I read about
in this book on the history of cacao:
it's in chocolate, they tell you,
and has beneficial influences on the moods,
the substance is the same the brain
releases in various doses
when you're angry or in love.
And if she knows nothing of this, Farida,
can the magpie know coming in to land
on the courtyard lawn and if it doesn't give a damn
about the wind making Ireland more alone,
more an island?

II

Bayside's calm tonight. It's stopped raining, someone's
taking the dog for a walk, the photoelectric cells
dazzle him passing by that point next door.
On marine parade tonight you see the whole bay, and Sandycove

e la collina di Dalkey con la brughiera di ginestre
dove ieri una coppia, seduta su massi pezzati di giallo lichene,
di spalle contro il cielo, come in un quadro di Friedrich,
contemplava la baia. Chi sapeva i nomi dei luoghi
con la mano spiegava il paesaggio, indicava
la sua casa lontana.

from Replica / Reply (2006)

and the hill of Dalkey with its broom heath
where yesterday a couple, sitting on boulders spotted with
                                                        yellow lichens,
backs against the sky, as in a Friedrich painting,
stared out to sea. The one who knew the place-names
explained the landscape with his hand, he pointed out
his house there in the distance.

SU UN SOSIA

Chissà chi è quello che si sbraccia e mi fa segno
e correndomi incontro con la furia
di un uomo di vent'anni mi saluta da lontano
e «don Giovanni», mi grida, «don Giovanni».
Mi scambia per un altro, ci scommetti? E infatti,
vedendo più da presso la mia faccia perplessa,
neanche troppo si scusa dell'inganno e giulivo
mi sorride: «Credevo che tu fossi
don Giovanni». «Ho capito», io gli dico,
«ma questo don Giovanni, mi scusi, ma chi è?»
«È il prete di Abbadia. Se lo conosco?
Eccome, quest'estate gli ho portato gli agoni
a don Giovanni, e te lo garantisco,
è proprio uguale a te».

E allora dài, su, andiamo ad Abbadia:
ho voglia di incontrarlo, di conoscerlo meglio
questo prete di lago, non di anguille ghiotto ma di agoni,
che la domenica tiene l'omelia
con la sua faccia al posto della mia.

from Replica / Reply (2006)

ON A DOUBLE

Who knows who it is who's waving and signalling to me
and running towards me with the hurry
of a twenty-year-old he greets me from afar
and 'Don Giovanni,' he cries, 'Don Giovanni.'
He's confused me with somebody else, you're betting? And in fact,
seeing my perplexed face more closely
not even too sorry for the delusion and gleeful
he smiles at me: 'I thought you were
Don Giovanni.' 'I got that,' I tell him,
'but this Don Giovanni, I'm sorry, who is he?'
'He's the priest at Abbadia. Do I know him?
Totally, this summer I took the shad
to Don Giovanni, and I guarantee,
he's really exactly like you.'

Well then, come on, let's go to Abbadia:
I want to meet him, to know him better,
this priest by the lake not greedy for eel but for shad,
who holds his sermons on a Sunday
with his face in place of mine.

POUR PRENDRE CONGÉ

Al venditore di pannocchie arrosto di Boulevard Barbès
(le cuoce su un fornello dentro un carrello del *supermarché*),
alla donna che nella fretta ha smarrito tre foto tessera
su un *composteur* della Gare de l'Est,
ai cinesi che sotto la Tour Eiffel
offrono *Vittel et coca et bièle*,
al bulgaro che suona musiche gitane nel *métro*
e poi fa la questua con l'astuccio degli occhiali,
alla ragazza ebrea dalle splendide sopracciglia nere
che gioca a dama col fratello e intanto gli parla inglese,
alle battone africane di Rue Labat, dove abito,
che passata la tempesta tornano in su la via,
a loro e a tanti altri come loro che si arrabattano,
o forse anche no, con tatto e cortesia dico: *adieu*.

from Replica / Reply (2006)

TO TAKE LEAVE

To the grilled sweetcorn seller of Boulevard Barbès
(he cooks them on a gas-ring in a supermarket trolley),
to the woman who in haste has mislaid three passport photos
on a composter at the Gare de l'Est,
to the Chinese under the Tour Eiffel
offering *Vittel* and *coca* and *bièle*,
to the Bulgarian playing gypsy music on the Metro
who then with his glasses-case makes the collection,
to the Jewish girl with splendid black eyebrows
playing Dama with her brother while addressing him in English,
to the African hookers of Rue Labat, where I live,
who after the rain storm return up the street,
to them and many like them who are muddling through,
or maybe not, politely and with tact I say: *adieu.*

BICICLETTE, GENERAZIONI

    I

Il posto è quello adatto, il piazzale antistante la scuola
il tempo un pomeriggio di un giorno che non piove
gli attori padri e figlie con loro biciclette

la mia mano si stacca dal sellino e la bici
lanciata nella corsa non vacilla
no, non cadi, pedala, non avere paura

    II

Mio padre tentò invano di insegnare
a suo padre ad andare in bicicletta, fu sul viale
della stazione di Greco Pirelli

forse intanto passava un treno merci oppure il treno
che portava al paese di mia madre
a trovarla mio padre ci andava in bicicletta

    III

Vedo il nonno Mariani, col cappello della domenica,
inforcare di slancio la sua bici da vedovo
attraversare il cortile fischiettando

andava a suonare ai vespri
solo negli ultimi anni si faceva accompagnare
in macchina da uno dei cantori

from Replica / Reply (2006)

BICYCLES, GENERATIONS

    I

The place is the right one, small square before the school
time one afternoon of a day without rain
actors dads and daughters with their bicycles

my hand's let go of the saddle and the bike
launched on its way doesn't wobble
you won't fall, pedal, no, don't be afraid

    II

My father tried in vain to teach
his father how to ride one, on the boulevard
of the Greco-Pirelli station it was

perhaps while a freight train passed or the train
that would take him to my mother's place
to meet there my father went by bike

    III

I see granddad Mariani, with his Sunday hat,
impetuously mounting his widower's bike
to cross the courtyard whistling

he was going to play for the vespers
only in his last years would he be taken
by one of the singers in a car

ANCORA VERSO MARINA

Là dove l'altra estate fu un ramarro
la preda ignara di un giorno felice
pensi agli amori che durano più delle dune,
alla cicala che ricicla il suo canto,
tutti gli anni lo stesso.
Nel sole-ombra dei pini pare immune
dagli sgarbi del tempo
il tuo gusto feroce dell'estate.

from Replica / Reply (2006)

ONCE MORE TOWARDS MARINA

There where the other summer a lizard was
one happy day's unsuspecting prey
you think of the loves that last longer than the dunes,
of the cicada recycling its song
every year the same.
In the pines' sun-shadow it seems immune
to the slights of time
your ferocious love of summer.

IN BOCCA DI MARE

«Non è libeccio, maestrale o scirocco:
questo è vento di terra
e non è caldo, è fuoco».

*

«D'estate qui non piove quasi mai
e l'erba è tutta smorta e pesticciata».

*

«S'è piantato l'alloro.
Non c'era posto, in questa poca terra,
per oleandri o pitosfori».

*

«Nell'interno si pota come altrove,
ma qui, in bocca di mare,
conta poco l'estetica:
qui il secco non si tocca perché il secco
salva il verde».

from Replica / Reply (2006)

FACING THE SEA

'It's not libeccio, mistral or scirocco:
this wind's from the land
and it's not hot, it's fire.'

    *

'It hardly ever rains here in summer
and the grass is all wan and trampled.'

    *

'The laurel's planted.
There wasn't any space, in this little ground,
for pitosporum or the oleander.'

    *

'Inland they're pruned as elsewhere,
but facing the sea here
aesthetics counts for little:
here the dry nobody touches as the dry,
it's what saves the green.'

CENA CON GECO, A MONTEPESCALI

Ha il colore ineffabile del tufo
il geco che sul muro apre di scatto
le micidiali mandibole, azzanna
la malcapitata falena e non gioca
come il gatto col topo,
la tiene immobile in bocca
per un minuto che pare infinito,
poi scappa via tra ciuffi di sassifraghe
lontano quanto basta
per masticarla in pace, al riparo
dagli sguardi indiscreti.

from Replica / Reply (2006)

SUPPER WITH GECKO, AT MONTEPESCALI

The gecko on the wall has
the tufa's ineffable colour, it sharply
opens its deadly mandibles, bites
the unlucky mayfly and won't play
like the cat with a mouse,
but holds it immobile in its mouth
for a minute that seems an infinity,
then through saxifrage tufts gets away
as distant as necessary
to chew it in peace, protected
from the prying gazes.

LEGGENDO LA SEGNALETICA STRADALE

Questa è una strada provinciale
con alberi in banchina,
questo è un comune denuclearizzato,
questa è una zona militare
con contorno di filo spinato.

E questo è un fondo chiuso,
questa un'area regolamentata
accessibile ai cani.
                (Quel cane,
più degli altri ramingo, mette il muso
fuori della rete, fa una rapida
sortita col suo pelo di randagio,
poi ringhia e rientra nei ranghi,
nell'area suddetta).

Se giri in bicicletta
e resti sulla pista per ciclisti,
non corri nessun rischio,
ma occorre stare attenti
alle radici emergenti.

from Replica / Reply (2006)

READING THE ROAD-SIGNS

This is a provincial highway
with trees at its edges,
this is a denuclearized town,
this a military zone
surrounded by barbed wire.

And this is private property,
this a regulated space
accessible to dogs.
                    (That dog,
bolder than the others, pokes its nose
out of the fence, it makes a quick
sally with its mongrel fur,
then barks and goes back to the ranks,
in the aforementioned space).

If you go around by bike
and stick to the cycle track
you're not at any risk,
but it's worth being aware
of the roots outcropping there.

COME L'ACQUA

Quel giorno che qualcuno mi spiegò
che l'acqua trova sempre la sua strada
(le vasche del giardino disegnavano
un arduo labirinto)
cominciai a sognare d'essere acqua
anch'io: oh, traboccare, tracimare,
e come l'acqua andare verso il mare.

from Replica / Reply (2006)

LIKE WATER

That day when one explained to me
how water always finds its way
(the garden pools were drawing
an intricate labyrinth)
I started to dream of being water,
me too: oh to flow over, to overflow
and like water go down to the sea.

da

LA CARTA DELLE ARANCE

(2016)

from

THE ORANGES' PAPER

(2016)

UN PAESAGGIO INVERNALE

'About suffering they were never wrong,
The Old Masters…'
      W. H. Auden, 'Musée des Beaux Arts' (1939)

Lo sapevano bene anche gli allievi
dei Vecchi Maestri fiamminghi:
tutto dipende dal punto
dove si posa lo sguardo.
Prendi Marten van Cleve, per esempio,
e il suo *Paesaggio invernale
con la Strage degli innocenti*.
L'occhio corre alle lance, agli elmi,
alle armature lucenti, al cane
che abbaia dietro ai soldati a cavallo,
mentre sulla sinistra, in basso, un fante
rinfodera la spada e un altro,
più giovane, poco più che un ragazzo,
tiene stretto un pugnale e ha sul volto
un'espressione strana e guardinga;
al centro, proprio nel mezzo, un terzo,
un cavaliere smontato di sella,
dirige contro il tronco d'un albero
un fiotto potente d'urina.
Questo vediamo,
perché c'è questo in primo piano.
Ma se aguzzi la vista,
qualcosa scorgi e ben altro intuisci
sullo sfondo e nella zona più in ombra:
le porte spalancate con violenza, gli armigeri
che fanno irruzione, lo strazio
delle madri a cui strappano i figli dal grembo,
gli infanti riversi al suolo, a braccia aperte,
a disegnare una croce … Eppure
non c'è traccia del rosso del sangue
sulla neve innocente, tutto il vermiglio

from La carta delle arance / The Oranges' Paper (2016)

A WINTER LANDSCAPE

'About suffering they were never wrong,
The Old Masters ...'
        W. H. Auden, 'Musée des Beaux Arts' (1939)

They also knew very well, the pupils
of the Flemish Old Masters:
it all depends upon the point
from where you place the view.
Take, for example, Marten van Cleve
and his *Winter Landscape*
with Massacre of the Innocents.
The eye goes straight to the lances, helmets,
to the shining armor, the dog
barking behind the soldiers on horseback,
while to the left, below, a foot-soldier
sheathes his sword and another,
younger, barely more than a boy
keeps tight hold of his dagger with a strange
and cautious expression on his face;
at the center, right in the middle, a third,
a horseman out of his saddle,
directs against the trunk of a tree
a powerful stream of his pee.
And this we see,
because there's this in the foreground.
But if you narrow your eyes,
you notice one thing and quite another intuit
in the depth, the area most in shade:
doors violently flung wide, the officers
making the break-in, the torment
of mothers from whose laps they tear the children,
the infants dumped on the ground, arms wide,
in the shape of a cross ... And yet
there's not a trace of the blood's red colour
on the innocent snow, the vermilion,

Marten l'ha steso uniforme
sulle casacche dei soldati e sugli stendardi
che garriscono al vento.
Anche questo vorrà dire qualcosa,
non pensi?

from La carta delle arance / The Oranges' Paper (2016)

Marten has spread it uniformly all
on the tunics of the soldiers and the standards
which are fluttering in the wind.
Even this will want to say something,
don't you think?

LUOGHI DA RIVISITARE

'...Intagliato in legno duro:
gli occhi sbarrati per lo spavento, solo facce che urlano,
un Inferno sulla punta di uno spillo, una piccola goccia, luccicante.
A fatica afferrabile, era lì, *in nuce*, condensato
quello che in avvenire sarebbe toccato alla città, come emblema...'
   Durs Grünbein, *Porzellan* (2005)

Nell'elenco sommario, indicativo,
c'era anche il bunker di fianco al Duomo,
«dove ora c'è il museo romano»,
e quel sobborgo di Colonia, Deutz,
sulla destra del Reno,
dove aveva abitato qualche tempo
in quell'inverno buio di tregenda:
«Era rimasta in piedi una sola casa
in Reischplatz», ma del resto tutta la città
era un enorme ammasso di macerie.
Per questo a sessant'anni da allora
si era messo a tradurre per sé
qualche verso d'un libro appena uscito
che parlava di Dresda rasa al suolo.
In quello specchio di parole tedesche
riconosceva se stesso, a vent'anni, testimone
della rovina scesa su Colonia,
su tanta fragile ricchezza umana.
 «Deutz», mi spiegava, «viene da *Divitia*».

from La carta delle arance / The Oranges' Paper (2016)

PLACES TO REVISIT

'...Cut into hard wood:
eyes bulging from fear, only howling faces,
an Inferno on a pinhead, a little drop, gleaming,
graspable with effort, there – *in essence* – it was condensed,
what in the future would touch the city – as emblem ...'
        Durs Grünbein, *Porzellan* (2005)

In the summary indicative list
there was even the bunker beside the Cathedral,
'where now there's the Roman museum,'
and Deutz, that suburb in Cologne,
on the right bank of the Rhine,
where he'd lived for some time
in that dark winter of the fire-storms:
'Only a single house left standing
in Reischplatz,' but for the rest the whole city
was an enormous heap of rubble.
That's why some sixty years later
he'd sat down to translate for himself
some lines from a book just out
that spoke of Dresden raised to the ground.
In that mirror of German words
he found himself, at twenty, witness
to the ruin befallen on Cologne,
on so much fragile human wealth.
'Deutz,' he explained, 'derives from *Divitia*.'

DI UN CAVALLO E DI UN CARRO

Al suo cavallo baio,
dalle poderose culatte,
dalla coda a frusta
terrore delle mosche vespertine,
il mugnaio Calistro
poneva sulle tempie
neri paraocchi di cuoio,
perché a quell'ora il suo ruolo
era tirare il carro
stracarico di sacchi di farina
bianca o gialla, per pane o per polenta,
non distrarsi a guardare
chi lo faceva adombrare:
noi, ad esempio,
pronti a saltare sul carro
e a farci portare come cowboy
dell'Arizona o dell'Ohio
almeno fino a quando,
terminate le consegne,
il mugnaio emetteva l'ultimo «arri!»
e noi si saltava giù in corsa,
prima che lui s'arrabbiasse per finta
o per davvero.

from La carta delle arance / The Oranges' Paper (2016)

OF A HORSE AND A CART

Upon his bay horse
with mighty hind-quarters,
with whip-like tail
the evening flies' terror,
Calistro the miller
would place at its temples
black leather blinkers,
because at that hour
his role was to pull
the cart overloaded with sacks
of white or yellow flour, for bread or polenta,
and not be distracted
looking at those who'd make him shy:
us, for example,
ready to jump up onto the cart
and make him bear us like cowboys
from Arizona or Ohio
at least as far as when,
consignments completed,
the miller would let out a final 'whoa'
and we would jump down at a run,
before he'd pretend to get angry
or do so for real.

INVENTARIO DEL BAGNO «ROSANNA»

C'era il forte sentore di salso
che ha il legno fradicio di mareggiata
se lo rasciuga il sole di luglio;
c'era l'impaccio della sabbia
rimasta sotto i sandali,
sulle stuoie e i teli da bagno;
c'era il caldo stagnante della cabina
con qualche sconnessura tra le pareti
tinteggiate di bianco e di blu;
c'era un riflesso di luce pomeridiana;
ma c'era sopratutto il tumulto
del sesso in risveglio.

from La carta delle arance / The Oranges' Paper (2016)

'ROSANNA' BATHING INVENTORY

There was the strong salty smell
that the wood had soaked by swell
if dried in the July sun;
there was the irritant sand
remaining under sandals,
on matting and bath towels;
there was the cabin's stagnant heat,
some loosening between the walls
painted in blue and in white;
there was a glare of afternoon light;
but there was the tumult most of all
of awakening to sex.

MADRIGALE PER A.

'When we moved I had your measure and you had mine.'
      Seamus Heaney

E poi il tornante dove abbandonarono
il Maggiolino Volkswagen celeste,
la radura nel bosco dove videro

la luna farsi sempre più tonda, meno rossa
nel cielo ad ogni istante più blu,
blu notte d'agosto,

e alla fine il corteo dei borghigiani,
con le torce e coi cani,
tutti accorsi a cercare i padroni

del Maggiolino Volkswagen celeste,
per paura che fossero caduti
nel dirupo, o si fossero perduti.

MADRIGAL FOR A.

'When we moved I had your measure and you had mine.'
    Seamus Heaney

And then the switchback where they left
their sky-blue VW Beetle,
the woodland clearing where they saw

the moon grown ever rounder, less red
in a sky at each instant more blue,
night-of-August blue,

and in the end the procession of locals,
with their dogs and torches,
all hurrying to search for the owners

of the sky-blue VW Beetle,
fearing they might have fallen
over the cliff, or lost their way.

PIÙ RAPIDA DEL DESIDERIO

Tutto accade così in fretta, e la luna
crescente che stampava sulla roccia rossastra,
verticale, le nostre silhouette affiancate
inarrestabilmente ora tramonta,
si fa minuscola, è un punto di luce,
una biglia di buio
che esplode.
         Non la vale
la miriade d'astri della notte d'agosto,
né quell'unica stella filante
che insieme abbiamo visto attraversare
un lungo tratto di cielo, fulminea, più rapida
del desiderio in cerca di parole.

from La carta delle arance / The Oranges' Paper (2016)

QUICKER THAN DESIRE

Everything happens in such a rush, and the moon
a crescent that prints on the reddish rocks,
vertical, our side-by-side silhouettes,
unstoppably now it sets,
grows tiny, is a point of light,
a marble of darkness
exploding.
          The myriad stars
in the August night count for naught,
nor that single shooting one
we had seen together crossing
a long sky-stretch, meteoric, much quicker
than desire in search of words.

GRAFFITI

Mi furono amiche,
quel giorno, le vertigini.
E così, mentre voi salivate
sull'Elevador de Santa Justa
per godere la vista
dalla terrazza più alta,
quella che da sola «vale il viaggio»,
io per fare qualcosa passavo il tempo
guardando i graffiti
accanto alla porta dell'ascensore,
leggendo le solite scritte in vari idiomi
con cuori e frecce, nomi e date,
I was here, I love you,
ma anche insulti e sfottò,
France – Brésil 3-0.
Solo ignoranti imbrattamuri, pensavo,
turisti incivili, scolari in gita, soldati in libera uscita?
O non anch'essi gente e basta, gente
senza aggettivi,
ma tutti con dentro un capogiro
a pensare di ripartire
senza lasciare un segno
che siamo stati qui?

from La carta delle arance / The Oranges' Paper (2016)

GRAFFITI

Friendly to me, that day,
were the vertigos.
And so, while you ascended
the Elevador de Santa Justa
to enjoy the view
from the highest terrace,
the one that's 'worth the visit' alone,
to do something, me, I passed the time
looking at graffiti
all around the lift door,
reading the usual inscriptions in different idioms
with hearts and arrows, dates and names,
I was here, I love you,
but taunts as well and insults
France 3 – Brésil nil.
Only ignorant wall-scribblers, I was thinking,
rude tourists, schooltrip kids, soldiers on furlough?
Or these too just people, people
without adjective,
but all with inside them a dizzying
thought of not going away
without leaving a sign
we have been here?

GENTE CHE PARLA

Laconico e scontroso, era un miracolo
se una volta su dieci ricambiava
il saluto dei passanti. Era selvatico,
dicevano: viveva solo, lavorava soltanto
se e quando ne aveva bisogno,
andava a caccia di frodo, metteva
le trappole per lepri e caprioli,
mangiava lumache, forse anche locuste
come il Battista.

Una volta che era giorno di festa,
mentre tutti facevano chiasso
e giocavano a tressette
dentro il fumo fitto dell'osteria,
un ragazzo osando gli chiese
perché lui non dicesse mai niente.
«Non ce n'è già abbastanza»
gli rispose «di gente
che parla?»

from La carta delle arance / The Oranges' Paper (2016)

PEOPLE WHO SPEAK

Terse and surly, a miracle it was
if he'd reply, one time in ten,
to the passersby's greeting. Wild,
he was, they'd say: he lived alone,
worked only if and when he had to,
went poaching, would put out
traps for hares and deer,
ate snails, perhaps even locusts
as had John the Baptist.

One time, one public holiday,
while all were making a din
and playing at *Tressette*
inside the thick hostelry smoke,
a boy dared ask him why
he wouldn't ever say a thing.
'Aren't there enough already,'
he'd come back, 'of people
who speak?'

LETTERA DA ZURIGO

Mentre qui fuori i merli
s'avventano sull'albero di sorbo
che allunga i rami a sfiorare il sambuco
e con avidità ne inghiottono le bacche scarlatte
prima di volar via, spaventati da un ombra,
mi viene in mente che volevo scriverti;
perché l'ultima volta che t'ho visto
m'hai snocciolato una serie di nomi di uccelli
in dialetto, tra cui i *finchi*, fringuelli
in italiano, *Finken* in tedesco,
ed io non ho potuto non pensare a Pascoli,
che tu forse non avevi mai letto.
Ma non importa: finché campo, con o senza merli
nei dintorni di sorbi o di sambuchi,
mi ricorderò di te, e dei *finchi*
e dell'ultima volta che t'ho visto.

from La carta delle arance / The Oranges' Paper (2016)

LETTER FROM ZURICH

Whilst outside here blackbirds
hurl themselves onto the rowan tree's
extended branches grazing the elder
and avidly swallow scarlet berries
before flying off, scared by a shadow,
it came to mind I wanted to write you;
because the last time I saw you
you'd rattled off a series of bird names
in dialect, among them the *finchi*, *fringuelli*
in Italian, *Finken* in German,
and I couldn't but think then of Pascoli,
whom maybe you hadn't ever read.
But no matter: so long as I live, with blackbirds
or without them near rowan or elder,
I'll think of you, and of the *finchi*
and of the last time that I saw you.

NEL PAESE DELLE FIABE

Nel recinto del vecchio cimitero
s'inseguono i bambini e le bambine,
scavalcano fiori secchi e granate tricolori
messe lì in piedi come granatieri,
fanno e rifanno un gaio girotondo
intorno al Monumento ai Caduti.
Ce n'è una, si chiama – ha detto – Alice,
sa le cose, le spiega agli altri, dice
che quelli sulle lapidi
«sono tutti pirati e capitani
che sono morti in guerra».
Il giorno dopo un altra, e questa è Anita,
ripassando davanti al Monumento
dice che lei «non è più tanto giovane»
(l'altro ieri ha compiuto quattro anni),
ma aggiunge, come per rassicurarmi,
che «i bambini non possono morire,
perché a morire sono solo i vecchi,
ma quelli proprio vecchi vecchi vecchi,
o quelli che c'erano tanto tempo fa,
o quelli che stanno lontano,
ma molto, molto lontano da qua».

from La carta delle arance / The Oranges' Paper (2016)

IN THE LAND OF FAIRYTALES

In the confines of the old cemetery
the small boys and girls follow each other,
they tread down dried flowers and tricolour grenades,
stood upright there like grenadiers,
they form and reform a gay ring-a-ring-a-roses
all round the Monument to the Fallen.
There's one, she's called – she said so – Alice,
who knows, explains to the others, she says
that those on the headstones
'they're all pirates and captains
who are dead in the war.'
The next day another, and this one's Anita,
going by again in front of the Monument,
she says she's 'no longer so young'
(she was four years old the other day),
but adds, as if to reassure me,
that 'the children, they can't die,
because dying's what only the old ones do,
but those really, really, really old,
or those who were a long, long time ago,
or those who are oh far away,
but very, very far away from here.

LA VICINA

Ha gli occhi rossi, la vicina, e dice
d'essersi accorta che lui stava male:
da giorni non sentiva il ticchettio
della macchina da scrivere.

Lei ci era abituata, a quel rumore:
«Ha scritto molto fino a poco tempo fa,
anche il suo stesso necrologio, ha detto Adele,
no, non il necrologio del giornale,

l'epitaffio, sì, insomma le parole
che metti sulla lapide.
L'ha fatto leggere ad Adele, e lei

gli ha detto: Mario, visto che ci sei,
scrivi anche il mio. E lui l'ha scritto. Poi
l'hanno portato lì, all'ospedale».

from La carta delle arance / The Oranges' Paper (2016)

THE NEIGHBOUR WOMAN

She's got red eyes, the neighbour, and says
how she's aware he wasn't well:
for days she hasn't heard
the tip-tapping of his typewriter.

Used to it, she'd grown, to that sound:
'He's written a lot right up to just now,
even his own obit, said Adele,
no, not the newspaper obituary,

the epitaph, yes, anyway the words
you put on the tombstone.
He'd got Adele to read it, and she,

she told him: Mario, seeing as you're here,
write mine too. And he'd written it. Then
they took him away, to the hospital.'

IL DISINCANTO E LA METRICA

'Now after so many years the other voice
doesn't remember and maybe believes I'm dead.'
        Eugenio Montale (trans. Harry Thomas)

A Heathrow, all'aeroporto,
per ingannare l'attesa
leggo un Montale tradotto in inglese,
e mi ritorna in mente l'altra estate

quando mio padre al telefono ha chiesto
se era arrivata posta,
ma non cose per lui senza importanza,
bollette della luce o resoconti della banca.

«Cartoline, per caso?»
Mi dispiace, dicevo, non c'è niente,
e allora ha pronunciato quella frase

che adesso mi ridico senza sosta
(«Si vede che mi credono già morto»),
perfetto endecasillabo di sesta.

from La carta delle arance / The Oranges' Paper (2016)

DISILLUSION AND METER

'Now after so many years the other voice
doesn't remember and maybe believes I'm dead.'
        Eugenio Montale (trans. Harry Thomas)

At Heathrow, in the airport,
to trick away the wait
I read a Montale in English translation,
and back to mind comes the other summer

when my father asked me on the phone
if there was any post arrived,
but not stuff of no importance to him,
electricity bills and bank statements.

'Postcards, for instance?'
No, sorry, I was saying, there's nothing,
and so he pronounced that phrase

which now I repeat to myself without cease
('You see they think that I'm already dead'),
a perfect pentameter with second-foot caesura.

MOMENTO DI TREGUA

I.

Il mostro è qui, la ruspa dalle chele d'acciaio,
dirocca i muri toccandoli appena,
si sposta provocando il maggior crollo
con il minimo sforzo.

Ora la casa è sventrata, a sezione verticale.
Niente a che vedere con *La Vie
mode d'emploi*, eppure anche qui
chi osserva dai balconi circostanti

indovina la forma delle stanze,
gli aloni sugli intonaci, l'intreccio
dei tubi dove l'acqua come il sangue
in un corpo saliva e discendeva...

II.

È un momento di tregua, la pausa delle nove.
Un vecchio, un uomo giovane, una donna,
tre bambini (chi sono?) vanno e vengono,

mettono in salvo gli infissi, le imposte,
il legno ancora buono, si dicono parole
che non colgo.

Torneranno tra poco gli operai dai caschi gialli,
s'aggireranno nel cortile controllando
lo stato dei lavori.

Demolito quanto resta, comincerà lo scavo.

A MOMENT'S TRUCE

    I.

The monster's here, the steel-clawed digger,
it knocks down walls with hardly a touch,
moves to provoke the greatest collapse
with the slightest force.

The house is gutted now, in vertical section.
Nothing to do with *La Vie*
mode d'emploi, even if here too
who watches from the balconies around

guesses the form of the rooms,
the rings on the plaster, the tangle
of pipes where the water like blood
in a body would rise and fall…

    II.

It's a moment's truce, the nine-o'clock pause.
An old man, a young one, a woman,
three children (who are they?), they come and go,

set to saving the fixtures, the frames,
the wood still good, say words
that I don't catch.

Soon they'll return, the workers in their yellow helmets,
will go round the courtyard checking
the state of progress.

Demolished what remains, they will start to excavate.

LINGUE IN TRANSITO

Passano le frontiere
insieme alle persone, sono leggere
come l'aria, come il respiro
di chi le parla. Non pagano
né dazio né dogana,
e nessuno può chiuderle in gabbia,
gettarci sopra la calce o la sabbia.

from La carta delle arance / The Oranges' Paper (2016)

LANGUAGES IN TRANSIT

They go across borders
with persons, they're
light as air, as the breath
of those who speak them. They
pay neither toll nor duty and
no one can cage them,
can cast on them the lime or sand.

RONDÒ DI CASTELSARDO

I gabbiani, dunque.
Per quanto tu resista
all'impulso di nominarli,
non c'è niente da fare:
è estate, tutto il giorno la finestra
è aperta e ad ora ad ora sopraggiungono
questi orgiastici gridi prolungati.

Ah, che vita da nababbo
ch'è quella del gabbiano:
nidifica sulle rocce a picco sul mare,
si fa portare dai venti,
che qui mai non restano,
e quando ha fame pesca
col becco non diritto ma neanche
troppo adunco.

from La carta delle arance / The Oranges' Paper (2016)

CASTELSARDO RONDO

The seagulls, then.
As much as you resist
the impulse to name them,
there's nothing you can do:
it's summer, the window is open
all day and from time to time come
these orgiastic extended cries.

Ah, what a jet-set lifestyle
is that of the seagull:
build nests on sheer cliffs by the sea,
be carried by the winds,
the ones that never rest here,
and when famished go fishing
with a beak not straight but not
too crooked either.

PER UN AMATORE DI GATTI

a Luciano Erba, in memoria

Se non avessimo per ben due volte
sbagliato strada fra Sihlbrugg e Zug,
ma stranamente senza prendercela né io né tu,
non avremmo mai visto quel gatto soriano
accoccolato nell'erba, sovrano assoluto del prato,
guardarci manovrare avanti e indietro senza costrutto:
due busti, quattro ruote, scarso fiuto.

from La carta delle arance / The Oranges' Paper (2016)

FOR A CAT LOVER

to Luciano Erba, in memory

If we hadn't as good as twice
mistaken the road between Sihlbrugg and Zug,
but strangely without either you or I taking it,
we'd never have seen that tabby cat
snuggling in the grass, absolute lord of the meadow,
watching us manoeuvre to no end back and forth:
two torsos, four wheels, little scent.

VIAGGIANDO VERSO IL MONFERRATO

con Mimma e Giorgio

Lo dici commovente
il rosso dei papaveri nei fossi,
lungo le carreggiate dei sobborghi di Pavia,
ai bordi delle risaie allagate
o che «aspettano l'acqua».
Lo stesso vale, in pensiero,
per il blu dei fiordalisi,
che dei papaveri condividono le sorti
regressive: falcidiati da pesticidi, diserbanti,
si rifugiano ai margini dei campi,
tra i ruderi, o scompaiono alla vista.
E con loro, è l'estate
che smarrisce i suoi colori.

JOURNEYING TOWARDS MONTFERRAT

with Mimma and Giorgio

You say it moves you
the poppies' red in the ditches,
down carriageways on the outskirts of Pavia,
at the sides of flooded rice fields
or those 'expecting water'.
The same is true, to think of it,
for the blue of the *fleur-de-lis*,
which shares the poppies' same regressive
fate: scythed down by pesticides, weed-killers,
they take refuge in field borders,
amidst ruins, or disappear from sight.
And with them, it's the summer
has mislaid its colours.

IL CIELO DI MAGGIO IN LOMBARDIA

Se l'avanguardia delle stelle estive
sorgerà verso est poco dopo il tramonto,
Mercurio brillerà come previsto
sull'orizzonte occidentale e Marte

sarà visibile tutta la notte,
splendidamente. Chi vorrà, vedrà
stelle cadenti, sciami
di meteoriti, polveri disperse

dalle comete...
Ma non è quello dell'astronomo
il tuo cielo di maggio, è questo cielo
che dilaga nel presente, identico a come era,

il cielo amico di tutti i nostri ieri
che torna nello sciame dei tuoi pensieri.

from La carta delle arance / The Oranges' Paper (2016)

MAY-TIME SKY IN LOMBARDY

If the avant-garde of the summer stars
climbs towards east a little after sunset,
Mercury will shine as foreseen
on the western horizon and Mars

be visible all through the night,
splendidly. Who would, will see
falling stars, showers
of meteorites, dispersed dusts

from comets…
But it isn't the astronomer's,
your May-time sky, it's this one
swelling in the present, quite as it was,

the friendly sky of all our yesterdays
come back in the shower of your thoughts.

IL POETA E IL MECENATE

Deve essere per forza un vate
il poeta che lui premia
e magari di un tipo un po' speciale,
sul rustico-ruspante,
uno che verso l'alba lascia il borgo
con schioppo e cartucciera
e al vespero rientra fischiettando
con fagiani o beccacce nel carniere.
Insomma, a sentir lui,
il vate è ancora lì che l'accarezza
la sua vecchia carabina.
Il poeta ringrazia, scuote il capo,
dice che d'acqua n'è passata sotto i ponti
e sopra i sassi:
«I tempi sono assai cambiati,
si parla tanto di pentiti e io sono,
se permette, un cacciatore pentito».
Chissà se l'ha capito,
il moderno Mecenate.

from La carta delle arance / The Oranges' Paper (2016)

THE POET AND MAECENAS

He's obliged to be a vates,
the poet he rewards
and maybe a type a bit special,
on free-range rustic lines,
one who leaves his village at dawn
with cartridge-belt and shotgun
and whistling at dusk returns
with pheasants and woodcock in his game-bag.
All in all, to hear him,
the vates is still there caressing
his old-time carbine.
The poet's grateful, shakes his head,
says enough water's gone under the bridges
and over the stones:
'The times are so changed,
much talk of penitents and me,
if you will, I'm a penitent hunter.'
Who knows if he has understood it,
your modern Maecenas.

PANCHINE ALLO ZOO

Ma poi perché sorridere
di questa strana voglia
di lasciare una targa in memoria
(*non omnis moriar*)
dove gli stanchi posteri
si mettono a sedere?
È forse la più dura delle sorti
sopravvivere in forma di panchina
lungo i viali dello zoo,
qui a Berlino o ad Anversa
o ad Anderswo?

from La carta delle arance / The Oranges' Paper (2016)

BENCHES AT THE ZOO

But then why smile
at this weird wish
to leave a plaque in memory
(*non omnis moriar*)
where, weary, the posteriors
set themselves to sit?
Is it maybe the hardest of fates
to live on in bench-form
down avenues at the zoo,
here in Berlin or in Antwerp
or in Anderswo?

AUGENLICHT

'...miro este querido
mundo que se deforma y que se apaga
en una pálida ceniza vaga...'
        Jorge Luis Borges, 'Poema de los dones'

I

È come stare dentro a un videogame,
e tu sei l'orso, il grizzly che prendono di mira;
a ogni colpo del laser che rattoppa,
un lampo verde, una fitta sottile.
Il microscopio fruga, mette a fuoco
la retina strappata e tu contempli
una landa lunare, una pianura tutta crepe:
poi pensare, se vuoi, ai cretti di Burri.

II

«L'occhio è un organo chiuso, ma *keine Angst*,
la lieve emorragia dovrebbe riassorbirsi».
Non si riassorbe, invece, ed ecco allora
cavallucci marini, ombre cinesi,
volatili figure nere e strane.
Mouches volantes? Macché,
piuttosto grossi corvi con le ali spiegate.
Tecnicamente, *eine massive Blutung*.

III

Una tenace pece
bluastra e gialla ingromma il cristallino:
se muovi il capo, se giri lo sguardo
tutto nell'occhio si mette a frullare
e una parte del mondo s'invola.
Quando appare una nuvola

from La carta delle arance / The Oranges' Paper (2016)

EYESIGHT

'...I look upon this dear
world that's deforming and fading
to a pallid ashen grey...'
        Jorge Luis Borges, 'Poem of the Gifts'

    I

It's like being inside of a videogame,
and you're the bear, the grizzly at whom they take aim;
at each strike of the laser, which patches,
a green light, a slight stab.
The microscope searches, focuses down
upon the torn retina and you survey
a lunar landscape, a plain all cracks:
then think, if you like, of Burri's *cretti*.

    II

'The eye's a closed organ, but *keine Angst*,
the small bleed will be reabsorbed.'
But it's not reabsorbed, and you see then
seahorses, Chinese shadows,
flying figures black and strange.
Mouches volantes? Not really,
more like great crows with splayed wings.
Technically, *eine massive Blutung*.

    III

A bluish and yellow
stubborn pitch encrusts the lens:
if you move your head, if you turn your gaze
everything in the eye begins to blur
and a part of the world is lost.
When a blackest, straggly

nerissima, sfrangiata,
e sotto, lungo l'orlo,
vedi lampi che corrono
per linee orizzontali,
non c'è tempo da perdere,
ora tocca al chirurgo.

    IV

Con grazia l'*Augenschwester*
ti libera la guancia dai cerotti, solleva
la conchiglia di plastica, la garza, dischiude
le ciglia ingombre di pomata e sangue:
meravigliosamente
tutto riprende il suo posto, il soffitto,
la finestra, le case, le colline
là dietro l'alta torre che s'arrampica
al cielo, a *Züri West*.

from La carta delle arance / The Oranges' Paper (2016)

cloud appears
and under, along the edge,
you see flashes running
in horizontal lines,
there's no time to lose,
it's the surgeon's turn.

IV

With grace the *Augenschwester*
frees your cheek from plasters, also
lifts the plastic shell, the gauze, she frees
the eyelids stuck with blood and ointment:
miraculously
everything returns to its place, the ceiling,
window, houses, the hills
there behind the high tower which climbs
the sky, in *Züri West*.

LA CASA DI KEATS

Tutto il dolore del cuore m'arriva
con la pioggia che cade e il verde così verde.
Su queste vecchie carte niente ravviva
la lettera triste che col tempo si perde.

Vuoto di te contemplo le stanze,
mi siedo al tuo posto nel *reading room*.
Niente attenua i rimpianti.
Non sento, dei tuoi anni, alcun profumo.

Furono vane le tue malattie
e le tante ore dolci di quei dì
con gli amici e Fanny nel giardino?

Non ci sono usignoli sul pruno,
la luce del sud sarà la luce estrema
– sorte migliore non spero per me.

(*da* Narcís Comadira)

from La carta delle arance / The Oranges' Paper (2016)

KEATS' HOUSE

All the aching of the heart arrives
with the falling rain and green so green.
On these old papers nothing revives
the sad letter that you lose with time.

Nothing attenuates the laments.
Empty of you, I ponder the space,
sat in the *reading room* at your place,
don't catch, from your years, any scents.

Were they vain, your illnesses
and the many sweet hours of your days
with friends and Fanny in the garden?

There are no nightingales on the plum-tree,
a southern light will be the last light
– no better fate do I hope for me.

(*from* Narcís Comadira)

UN POSTO COSÌ

«Pieno inverno non era, e neanche inizio primavera,
tardo autunno piuttosto, come verso Sant'Ambrogio,
e il posto era un posto così, Briosco o Inverigo,
dove spesso si andava tutti insieme
per portarvi un po' fuori.

Vi sentivo rincorrervi in mezzo alla brughiera,
lungo quell'ansa del fiume – era il Lambro? –
che si copriva di un velo di nebbia innocua,
ben diversa dall'altra umida e nera
che da bambina chiamavo *scighera*.

Mi sembrava di vedervi scomparire e riapparire
tra l'intrico dei rami e l'erba magra,
scorgevo i vostri baveri rialzati, già pensavo
alle scarpe infangate da lustrare la sera.

Ma non so dire se eravate proprio voi perché gli strilli
mi parevano quelli della Lucia e del Giancarlo,
di quando correvamo noi su quello stesso prato
e il Giancarlo ad un tratto era sparito chissà dove

e io restavo lì con la Lucia a chiamarlo e chiamarlo,
che non andasse lontano, e alla fine era lei
che mi cercava e io non rispondevo,
sentivo la sua voce, ma dov'ero?...»

from La carta delle arance / The Oranges' Paper (2016)

SUCH A PLACE

'Mid-winter it wasn't, nor start of spring,
more likely late autumn, towards Sant'Ambrogio,
and the place was just such a place, Briosco or Inverigo,
where often we'd all go together
to take you outside a while.

I sensed you chase each other in the middle of the heath,
along that loop of river – was it the Lambro? –
covered in a veil of innocuous fog,
very different from that other damp and black
from childhood I would call *scighera*.

It seemed to me I saw you vanish and reappear
amongst the tangle of branches and thin grass,
I'd notice your collars turned up, would think already
on the muddy boots to clean that evening.

But I can't say was it really you all since the cries
seemed to be those of Lucia and Giancarlo,
from when we ran ourselves on that same meadow
and Giancarlo of a sudden disappeared who knows where

and I stayed there with Lucia calling and calling him,
who didn't go far, and in the end it was she
who was looking for me and I didn't reply,
I heard her voice, but where was I?...'

CHARLOT

«L'orologiaio di via della Spiga
era buffo perché camminava così...».
E si mise a imitarlo
tirandosi su i pantaloni con le mani in tasca,
come uno magro che debba andarsene in giro
con delle brache non sue, *extra large*,
senza avere cintura né bretelle.
Fu l'unica volta che vidi in mio padre
un uomo nato negli anni di Charlot.

CHARLIE

'The watchmaker in Via della Spiga
was funny 'cause he walked like this...'
And he made to imitate him,
hitching up his trousers, hands in pockets,
like a skinny man who has to go round
in britches not his own, *extra large*,
not having either belt or braces.
It was the one time I saw in my father
a man born in Charlie Chaplin's era.

UNA DELLE DIECI

Lo dice Sanguineti nelle sue *Postkarten*:
di un uomo se va bene si ricordano dieci frasi
e questi, dice, sono i casi fortunati.

Quel giorno uscendo per andare a un funerale
si era visto nello specchio dell'ascensore
(sempre più scavate
le guance, sempre più affilato il profilo)
e aveva detto solo:
io vengo come simbolo.

Non ci voleva meno dell'esperienza di una vita
(e di infinite letture) per arrivare a dire
in modo così elegante una verità tanto straziante.

from La carta delle arance / The Oranges' Paper (2016)

ONE OF THE TEN

It's Sanguineti who says in his *Postkarten*:
if all goes well of a man they remember ten phrases
and these, he says, are the fortunate ones.

That day on the way out to go to a funeral
he saw himself in the mirror of the lift
(even more hollowed out
the cheeks, ever more chiseled the profile)
and he'd said only:
I'm going as a symbol.

No less than a lifetime's experience you need
(and infinite reading) finally to utter
in so elegant a way such a wrenching truth.

IPOTESI SULL'ULTIMO SOGNO

Chissà se in sogno hai rivisto anche tu
il lento Eufrate fangoso o l'uccello
sulla grondaia, più snello d'un piccione e col ciuffo
arruffato dal vento. O magari nel buio

imperfetto dell'ultima notte è ricomparsa
per te la trota nera di Reading col suo luccichio
di carbonchio, s'è alzata a volo un'anitra
nera dal fondolago. Ti aveva letto dei versi

di Montale uno dei figli, la penultima sera,
e allora sì, tutto questo è possibile,
non è ridicolo crederlo. O forse invece nel chiaro

della primalba hai sognato di nuovo quel giorno
felice, e nel sonno, se anche nessuno sentiva,
di nuovo le hai detto: «Siamo a Sanremo, cara».

from La carta delle arance / The Oranges' Paper (2016)

SURMISES ABOUT THE LAST DREAM

Who knows if you revisited dreaming, you too,
the sluggish, muddy Euphrates or the bird
on the gutter, thinner than a pigeon and with tuft
ruffled by the wind. Or perhaps in the imperfect

darkness of that last night, the black trout
of Reading reappears with carbuncular
glitter, a black duck's uplifted in flight
from the lake floor. One of your sons had read

those lines of Montale's to you, that last evening,
and so then, yes, all this is possible,
it's not mad to believe it. Or perhaps instead

in the clear of early dawn again you dreamt
that happy day, and in sleep, though no one heard,
again you said it: 'We're in San Remo, dear.'

LA CARTA DELLE ARANCE

'e con ardente affetto il sole aspetta'
        Dante, *Paradiso* XXIII, 8

Quella carta velina, variopinta,
frusciante tra le dita
di chi la distendeva, la stirava con cura,
specie negli angoli, per innalzare
sotto i nostri occhi un fragile cilindro,
una precaria torre e poi incendiarla
con uno zolfanello, sulla cima;
e noi che aspettavamo intenti
di vederlo, quel sole di Sicilia
stampato sulla carta, sollevarsi
dal piatto con scrollo leggero
tramutantesi poi in volo tremulo –

ma più saliva più si consumava,
e, rimasto un istante sospeso nell'aria,
ecco un pezzo di sole annerito,
un frammento di torre in fiamme
ricadere sul piatto;
e allora, mentre ancora volteggiavano
sopra di noi coriandoli di carta strinata,
anche senza più fame
chiedevo un'altra arancia da sbucciare,
imploravo di rifarlo, ripeterlo,
quel gioco col fuoco.

from La carta delle arance / The Oranges' Paper (2016)

THE ORANGES' PAPER

'and she waits for the sun with warm feeling'
    Dante, *Paradiso* XXIII, 8

That tissue paper, vari-coloured,
rustling between the fingers
of whoever spreads it, irons with care,
especially at corners to raise
a fragile cylinder under our eyes,
a tottering tower, then set it on fire
up at the top, with a match;
and us intently waiting
to see it, that Sicilian sun
printed on the paper, lift
over the plate with faint shiver
changing then in tremulous flight –

but the higher it rose the more it was burned,
and, staying an instant suspended in air,
look, a piece of blackened sun,
a fragment of tower in flames
falling back onto the plate;
and then, while there still twirled around
charred paper confetti above us,
now not even hungry
I'd ask for one more orange to peel,
beg to repeat it, to do it again,
that playing with fire.

INEDITI

(2021)

UNCOLLECTED

(2021)

L'IGNOTO DI WATERLOO

'...Waterloo! morne plaine!'
    Victor Hugo

«Posso capire gli sforzi che fanno
per darmi un nome, uno scampolo
d'identità. Ma a chi importa davvero
se il mio corpo fu quello
d'un soldato di Hannover o quello d'un altro
come me, anche lui come me
solo carne mandata al macello?
Considerate invece le ossa ignude
sottratte alla terra che le albergò,
ricomposte con cura e ora esposte
alla vista di tutti, quasi fossi
una mummia egizia oppure Ötzi,
l'uomo dei ghiacci.
Considerate il cucchiaio di ferro
che mi servì forse più del moschetto,
e fra le costole la palla di piombo
che mi consegnò alla mia sorte.
Non ricordo più nulla di quel giorno,
né il lampo dei manipoli né l'onda
dei cavalli. Sono uno come tanti,
senza più patria ormai e senza nome.
Morti siamo, vivi fummo
e questo è tutto, proprio tutto
quel che c'è da sapere...»

THE UNKNOWN SOLDIER OF WATERLOO

'…Waterloo! dismal plain!'
        Victor Hugo

'I can understand the efforts they make
to give me a name, a remnant
of identity. But whom does it matter to, really,
if my body was that of a soldier
from Hanover or of another
like me, him too like me
just meat sent to the slaughter?
Consider rather the naked bones
drawn from the earth that gave them shelter,
recollected with care and exposed now
to everyone's view, as though I were
an Egyptian mummy or Ötzi,
the man of the ice.
Consider the teaspoon of iron
that served me maybe more than the musket,
and between my ribs the leaden ball
which consigned me to my fate.
I no longer remember a thing of that day,
neither flash of the company
nor cavalry wave. I was one like many,
with a homeland or name now no more.
The dead we are, the living we were
and that's all, really all
of what there is to know…'

NOTIFICHE DOPO L'INCENDIO

Anche il paesaggio, lo sai,
va letto in chiave darwiniana.
Sul sentiero che sale a Punta Baffe
registri tronchi di pini anneriti,
eriche rade e corbezzoli sparsi;
più sopra, in cresta, un filare di acacie
e dappertutto distese di felce aquilina.
Ma scendendo più giù, nelle vallette
dove non tutto è ridotto in cenere,
ecco la rara euforbia a doppia ombrella
e l'asfodelo, la pianta calunniata,
il fiore che non trema
al passaggio del fuoco.

Inediti / Uncollected (2021)

REPORTS AFTER THE FIRE

Even the landscape, you know,
gets read in Darwinian key.
On the path that climbs to Punta Baffe
you take in blackened trunks of pine,
thin gorse, few strawberry trees,
higher, on the ridge, a line of acacias
and everywhere spread with aquiline fern.
But going down further, into the groves
where not all's reduced to ashes,
look, the rare spurge with double umbrella
and the asphodel, the slandered plant,
the flower that doesn't tremble
at the passage of the fire.

LEZIONE DI SCRITTURA

a Fabio Pusterla

L'homo faber sa fare le cose:
taglia i tronchi alla giusta stagione,
li sfronda e con la stroppa
stringe le fascine,
poi sfende i ciocchi per ridurli in schiampe
da sistemare in luogo riparato,
contro il muro di casa che guarda a occidente
dove il sole d'estate dura a lungo
e la legna più verde
ha il tempo d'asciugare
mentre la poca resina rimasta sulla scorza
profuma l'aria di bosco.
Impara allora anche tu: metti in fila le parole
e ogni frase al suo posto,
come i pezzi di legna
della catasta.

WRITING LESSON

to Fabio Pusterla

Homo faber knows how to do things:
to cut trunks in the right season,
de-branch them and with the sling
tighten the bundles,
then cut up the blocks to reduce them to logs
for tidying into a sheltered spot,
against the house-wall that looks to the west
where the summer sun stays long
and the greener wood
has time to dry
while the little resin left in the bark
perfumes the woodland's air.
Then you too learn: you line up words,
each phrase in its place,
like the pieces of wood
in the log-pile.

IL FAGGIO DI MIO PADRE

«Là in fondo, una volta, c'era un pino...»
In verità era un peccio, cioè un abete rosso,
ma un giorno dovette farlo abbattere:
troppo cresciuto, era un pericolo per i vicini.

Piantò allora al suo posto un faggio,
più discosto dal muro del giardino.
Ora si erge maestoso e a maggio
è già così carico di fronde

che più tardi, alla fine dell'autunno,
sembrerà che ai suoi piedi si radunino
tutte quante le foglie del mondo.

Veniva qui a leggere, *sub tegmine fagi*.
Non aveva bisogno d'altro,
aveva i sui libri e l'ombra del faggio.

MY FATHER'S BEECH TREE

'There in the back, at one time, was a pine…'
In truth it was a spruce, that is, a red fir,
but one day it had to come down:
too grown, a risk to the neighbours.

Then in its place he planted a beech,
more distant from the garden wall.
Now it rises majestic and in May
it's already so laden with fronds

that much later, at the autumn's end,
it'll seem at its feet to have convened
the whole of this world's leaves.

He'd come to read, *sub tegmine fagi*,
had no need for anything else
with his books and that beech's shade.

PARLARE A UNA STATUA

Così assorta nel lutto, così mesto
il tuo volto benché senza pianto,
così fini le mani, così mossi i panneggi
della veste, del velo, e che lusso
gli orecchini pendenti, tempestati
di perle o rubini.
     (Essere
di marmo candido e adorno d'intagli
non cancella il dolore, anzi lo eterna.)

Non so nulla di te, di com'eri,
di come parlavi, se in lingua
o in dialetto, se il Porta leggevi
o il Manzoni o solo il tuo libro
delle orazioni.
     Non sono Gozzano,
non posso dire «rinasco, rinasco
del mille ottocento cinquanta!»,
ma ogni volta che torno
– porto un fiore qui accanto –
mando un saluto veloce anche a te,
vedovile figura che non vede
chi viene e chi va.

SPEAKING TO A STATUE

So distracted in grief, your face
so sad even if without tears,
so fine the hands, so swirled
the clothes, drapery, veil, and how rich
your earrings dangling, encrusted
with rubies and pearls.
                    (To be
of white marble and adorned in carving
won't delete sorrow, but make it eternal.)

I know nothing of you, how you were,
how you spoke, if in received
or dialect, if you'd read Porta,
Manzoni, or your book
of prayers only.
                    Not Gozzano,
I can't say, 'Born again,
I'm born again in eighteen fifty!',
but each time returning
– bringing a flower near here –
I give a quick salute to you too,
widow-figure that doesn't see
who comes and who goes.

SU UNA FOTOGRAFIA DI EMMY ANDRIESSE

(Sestri Levante, 1950–51)

«Per distinguermi da altre Marie,
la gente del borgo mi chiamava Maria la greca.

Scendevo ogni mattina alla spiaggia,
quando gli uomini tornavano dalla pesca notturna.

Anche se non era stata abbondante,
mi regalavano sempre un vassoio d'acciughe.

Finché un giorno una signora elegante
mi chiese di posare per lei.

La guardai con occhi incantati,
nessuno mai mi aveva fatto una fotografia all'aperto.

Mi disse di stare ferma così, con il mare alle spalle
e con in mano il vassoio delle acciughe.

Non sapevo chi fosse quel pittore
di cui parlava mentre armeggiava con l'apparecchio.

Uno che dipingeva ragazze come me, disse,
ma se lattaie o lavandaie ora bene non ricordo.

Forse disse proprio anche una ragazza come me
quel giorno, col fazzoletto in testa e gli orecchini.»

ON A PHOTOGRAPH BY EMMY ANDRIESSE

(*Sestri Levante, 1950–51*)

'To distinguish me from other Marias,
the townsfolk called me Maria the Greek.

Each morning I'd go down to the beach,
when the men returned from night-fishing.

Even if it hadn't been abundant,
they'd always let me have a tray of anchovies.

Until an elegant woman one day
asked me would I pose for her.

I looked at her with spellbound eyes,
no one had ever done my photo in the open.

She told me to stand still like this, the sea at my back
and a tray of the anchovies in my hands.

I didn't know who that painter could be
who she spoke of while she fumbled with the camera.

One, she said, who painted girls like me,
but if milkmaids or washerwomen I don't well remember.

Perhaps she really did say a girl like me
that day, with headscarf and earrings.'

LE CASE, LE COSE

a Valeria, che ascoltava

«Ma come, non ti ricordi
della nostra altra casa?»

Il vecchio discorreva,
e all'improvviso dentro le sue frasi
s'apriva uno iato, un pertugio, uno spioncino
che dava su un interno surreale
dove un corridoio era una lunga scala
e una casa stava dentro un'altra casa.

Erano tutte le case della sua vita
                    in una,
una costruzione più bizzarra delle cupe *Carceri*
di Piranesi, delle architetture impossibili
di Escher.

Il vecchio discorreva,
e dalla sua bocca uscivano, come fumetti nell'aria,
i suoi pensieri tristi e terminali: «E poi
dovrete decidere che cosa fare
di tutte le mie cose,
quelle che resteranno in questo mondo».

Inediti / Uncollected (2021)

THE HOUSES, THE THINGS

to Valeria, who was listening

'But how come, you don't remember
that other house of ours?'

The old man was reflecting,
and suddenly in his phrases
a gap opened, an aperture, a spyhole
giving onto a surreal interior
where a corridor was a long staircase
and a house was inside another.

There were all the houses in his life
                              in one,
a construction more dismal than Piranesi's
Carceri, or Escher's impossible
architectures.

The old man was reflecting,
and from his mouth came, like comic-strips in air,
his sad and final thoughts: 'And then
you'll have to decide what to do
with all these things of mine,
those that remain in this world.'

COME LA PANTERA DI RILKE

'Ihm ist, als ob es tausend Stäbe gäbe
und hinter tausend Stäben keine Welt.'
    Rainer Maria Rilke, 'Der Panther'

Nella vita fuori, dicono, faceva il guardaboschi,
con il sole o con la pioggia tutto il giorno all'aria aperta.

Ma ora ha la mente in disordine, la memoria a brandelli,
non dice una parola, non parla più a nessuno.

Solo cammina, tutto il giorno cammina,
avanti e indietro, e non si ferma mai.

Chissà che cosa pensa quando arriva all'inferriata,
guarda fuori, si volta, poi riprende il suo giro.

Rivedrà le sue piante, le sane e le malate,
gli abeti d'alto fusto, i sentieri interrotti nel bosco?

O vedrà anche lui solo sbarre e cancelli, sbarre e cancelli,
e nessun mondo fuori di qui?

LIKE RILKE'S PANTHER

'It's as if at a thousand bars he stares
and behind the thousand bars, no world.'
          Rainer Maria Rilke, 'Der Panther'

In the life outside, they say, he was a forest-ranger,
whether sunshine or rain in the open air all day.

But now his mind's disordered, his memory in tatters,
he doesn't say a word, no longer speaks to anyone.

He only walks, he walks all day,
forward and back, and never stops.

Who knows what he thinks when he reaches the grille,
he looks out, he turns, then takes up his round.

Will he see his plants once more, the healthy and the sick,
the beech with tall trunk, interrupted woodland ways?

Or will he too see only bars and gates, bars and gates,
and no world here beyond?

FINALE DI PARTITA

Recitano ancora la vita di ieri,
ciascuno la sua parte.
Sono le ultime battute di un film lunghissimo,
eppure così breve.

Poi verranno i titoli di coda, i *credits*
della colonna sonora, gli interminabili
ringraziamenti a tutti quanti, compresi i sarti
e i parrucchieri.

Inediti / Uncollected (2021)

END OF GAME

Still they're recounting yesterday's life,
each one with his own part.
They're the final lines of a very long film,
even if ever so short.

Then will appear the final titles, the *credits*
for the sound track, the interminable
thanks to one and all, not excluding the tailors
and the hairdressers.

CASCHI PURE IL MONDO

Come sorte dal nulla
dietro di noi delle voci infantili
e un *dlìn dlìn* argentino e ripetuto: tre bambine
col casco e lo zainetto dell'asilo
impazienti sulle loro *trottinettes*
ci chiedevano di scansarci, *dlìn dlìn*
non intralciare la loro corsa spensierata

Quando poi le abbiamo viste allontanarsi
rimpicciolire per la distanza
al di là dell'incrocio dove abbiamo svoltato
per tornarcene a casa
le abbiamo immaginate ancora allegre
così, col piede a mezz'aria
nel duemilacento o giù di lì

E allora anche noi
ci siamo detti *dlìn dlìn, dlìn dlìn*
caschi pure il mondo
noi oggi siamo qui

GO LET THE WORLD TUMBLE

How out of nothing behind us
there appear infant voices
and a silvery, repeated *ding ding*: three children
with helmet and kindergarten satchel
impatient on their scooters
they'd ask us to get out of the road, *ding ding*
not to impede their carefree way

When later we've seen them grow more remote
become smaller over the distance
beyond the crossroads where we'd turn
to get ourselves back home
we'd imagine them still happy
thus, with a foot in mid-air
in twenty-one hundred or thereabouts

And well then even us
we've said *ding ding, ding ding*
go let the world tumble
us, today, we're here

NOTES

The following annotations were made with the gratefully acknowledged help of Pietro De Marchi. They are also much indebted to the notes in *Here and not Elsewhere: Selected Poems 1990-2010* trans. Marco Sonzogni (Toronto: Guernica Editions, 2012) and in *Das Orangenpapier / La carta delle arance* trans. Christoph Ferber (Zurich: Limmat Verlag, 2018).

Da *Parabole smorzate* (1999) / From *Stunned Parables*

Parabole smorzate / Stunned Parables
The poem's title conveys its metaphorical purpose by punning on 'parabolas' and 'parables', an ambiguity not preservable in English.

Capriccio / Capriccio
The title refers to Goya's series of etchings from the late eighteenth century including the famous one inscribed with the Spanish phrase, 'The sleep of reason breeds monsters'.

Con Valentina, dalle anatre / With Valentina, at the Ducks
Valentina De Marchi is the poet's daughter.

Una pagina di cielo / A Page of Sky
Marco Sonzogni notes that this was a common exercise in Italian primary schools by which children would write out a page of the word *cielo* (sky) and a page of the word *cieco* (blind).

Foto di paesaggio con figure / Landscape Photo with Figures
The poem is set in the town of Bergen-aan-Zee in northern Holland.

Verso Marina / Towards Marina
Marina di Grosseto is a seaside town in the Maremma, an area largely in Tuscany that spills over the border into Lazio. Sonzogni notes the literary pedigree of the green lizard (il ramarro), citing both *Inferno* 25, 79–81 and the ninth of Montale's 'Motetti' from *Le occasioni*.

Lisbona, Rua Garrett / Lisbon, Rua Garrett
Café A Brasileira is at 120 Rua Garrett, in the Chiado district of Lisbon. There is a bronze statue of the poet Fernando Pessoa (1888–1935) sitting outside it.

All'angolo di Freiestrasse / At the Corner of Freiestrasse
Freiestrasse (Free Street) is in Zurich, not far from where the poet lived when the

poem was written. The first direct-speech quotation is from *Inferno* 31, line 67, and is Nimrod, the builder of the Tower of Babel's cry. Its meaning, commenting on the effect of that hubris, perhaps, is uncertain. The second phrase in German means 'Are you a Jew?'

Frontespizio / Frontispiece
The epigraph is from Fernando Pessoa's 'Liberdade' (1935) and means 'Books are paper painted with ink'.

Gabbiani e folaghe / Seagulls and Coots
Migros is the name of a supermarket chain in Switzerland where, doubtless, the woman in the poem has purchased the bread she is scattering on the waters of the river Limmat in Zurich.

Promesse da marinaio / Promises from Sailors
The second stanza references Italo Svevo's third novel, *La coscienza di Zeno* (Confessions of Zeno), first published in 1923, in which, while telling his story as a form of therapy, the central character also attempts to give up smoking, endlessly lying to himself about his 'last cigarette'.

Rime baciate / Kissing Rhymes
The original's title is the standard term used for rhyming couplets in Italian.

Spiaggia libera / Free Beach
Stretches of beach in Italian seaside resorts are privately owned and space in them, along with deckchairs and sunshades, is rented out. A 'spiaggia libera' is a beach where you do not have to pay to sunbathe.

Da *Replica* (2006) / From *Reply*

Una sovrapposizione per Giampiero Neri / An Overlay for Giampiero Neri
The poet Gianpiero Neri (b. 1927) published his essay, 'Sovrapposizione di storia e natura nella ricerca letteraria' (Overlay of history and nature in literary research) in 2002.

Lettera da Binz / Letter from Binz
Fabio Pusterla (b. 1957) is an Italian-speaking Swiss poet and translator. Binz is a small village to the west of Zurich.

Davanti alla Pinacoteca / In Front of the Art Museum
The poem's events take place on 7 July 2005. The gallery is the Brera in central

Milan. The Golden Section is a principle of aesthetic proportion identified by Luca Piacioli in his *La divina proporzione* (1497). The epigraph is from Auden's 1938 poem inspired by Pieter Breughel's *Landscape with the Fall of Icarus* at the art gallery in Brussels which gives his poem its title.

Anni Settanta / The Seventies
The poem's epigraph is from the introduction to Manzoni's play, *Il conte di Carmagnola* (1820). The Arengario arches and piazza Diaz are in the centre of Milan, near the Duomo.

Attraversando la Polonia / Crossing Poland
The epigraph from Primo Levi's *The Truce* reads '...far off Krakow's belltowers redden.' 'O' is the initial of Oświęcim, the Polish name for Auschwitz. De Marchi translates the poem's penultimate line in Polish, which figures in *The Truce*, in its final one.

Promemoria da un luogo di betulle / Memo from a Place of Birches
The title refers to the small Polish town of Brzezinka, Birkenau in German, where the Nazi concentration camp was built. The poem also alludes to *Promemoria* (1994) by Luigi Meneghello (1922–2007), who was a Professor of Italian Literature at the University of Reading. The dedicatee of the poem is Katia Bleier Meneghello, the writer's wife, who survived transportation to Auschwitz and Bergen-Belsen, being liberated by the Allies in 1945.

Funerale a Baar / Funeral at Baar
Baar is a village in the Canton of Zug in Switzerland. The Latin phrases cited in the poem are from St Paul's First Letter to the Corinthians, 12–13: 'For now we see through a glass, darkly; but then face to face: now I know in part; but then shall I know even as also I am known.'

Qui e non altrove / Here and not Elsewhere
The Resegone is a range in the northwestern Italian Alps. Its name deriving from the similarity of its nine peaks to a saw-blade is explained in the opening page of Manzoni's *I promessi sposi* (The Betrothed).

Variazioni su un tema antico / Variations on an Old Theme
The old theme is François Villon's in his 'Ballade des dames du temps jadis' which begins 'Dites moi ou, n'en quel pays / Est Flora la belle Romaine...' (Tell me where, in what land / Is Flora the beautiful Roman girl) and has the famous refrain 'Mais ou sont les neiges d'antan?' (Where are the snows of yesteryear).'

Notes

Diario d'Irlanda / Ireland Diary
The poem was written in 2002 during the poet's visit to Ireland. Bayside, Sandycove and Dalkey are all along the coast of Dublin Bay.

Su una sosia / On a Double
Abbadia Lariana is a town in the province of Lecco on the shores of Lake Como.

Biciclette, generazioni / Bicycles, Generations
The Greco-Pirelli station is in the north of Milan.

Pour prendre congé / To Take Leave
Boulevard Barbès and the Rue Labat are in the 18th arrondissement of Paris, which includes the area of Montmartre.

Ancora verso Marina / Once more towards Marina
See the note for 'Verso Marina /Towards Marina' above.

Cena con geco, a Montepescali / Supper with Gecko, at Montepescali
Montepescali is a small town near Grosseto in Southern Tuscany.

Da *La carta delle arance* (2016) / From *The Oranges' Paper*

Un paesaggio invernale / A Winter Landscape
Marten van Cleve's painting is a work in oil on panel dated 1570 from a private collection in Belgium.

Luoghi da rivisitare / Places to Revisit
The poet's father made the Italian prose rendering of the lines cited from Grünbein's poem from his 2005 *Porzellan*.

Madrigale per A. / Madrigal for A.
The epigraph is the last line from Seamus Heaney's 'Tate's Avenue' in *District and Circle* (2006).

Graffiti / Graffiti
The 'Elevador de Santa Justa' is a sightseeing attraction in Lisbon.

Lettera da Zurigo / Letter from Zurich
The poem by Giovanni Pascoli (1855–1912) the poet couldn't help thinking of is 'Il fringuello cieco' (The Blind Finch) of 1903.

La vicina / The Neighbour Woman
The poem relates to the death in 2008 of Mario Zambarbieri, a Homer specialist and longtime teacher of Latin and Greek at the Liceo Carducci in Milan.

Il disincanto e la metrica / Disillusion and Meter
The epigraph and prompt for the poem is Harry Thomas's translation of 'A tarda notte' (Late at Night) from Montale's *Satura* (1971) to be found in *The Faber Book of 20th-Century Italian Poems* ed. Jamie McKendrick (London: Faber & Faber, 2004).

Momento di tregua / A Moment's Truce
Georges Perec's *La Vie mode d'emploi* (1978) is a novel that explores the lives of people living in the same Paris apartment building.

Rondò di Castelsardo / Castelsardo Rondo
Castelsardo is a town in the northwest of Sardinia in the province of Sassari.

Per un amatore di gatti / For a Cat Lover
The poems of Luciano Erba (1922–2010) include a number that take cats as their subject. Sihlbrugg is a village on the border between Canton Zug and Canton Zürich in Switzerland.

Viaggiando verso il Monferrato / Journeying towards Montferrat
Montferrat is an area in northwestern Italy between Piedmont and Liguria. Pavia is the city near Milan surrounded by rice fields. Giorgio and Mimma Orelli are the Swiss poet and his wife.

Il poeta e il mecenate / The Poet and Maecenas
The poet referred to here is Giorgio Orelli, who in his youth was also a hunter, and who has written a number of hunting poems.

Panchine allo zoo / Benches at the Zoo
'*non omnis moriar*' means 'not everyone dies' (cfr. Horace, *Odes*, III.30.6), while 'Anderswo' is the German for 'elsewhere', being used as if it were a place-name here.

Augenlicht / Eyesight
Alberto Burri (1915–1995) was an abstract painter who used unusual materials to create highly textured collages. He began his series of 'cracked' paintings, 'cretti', in the 1970s. 'Keine Angst' means 'don't worry' here. 'Mouches volantes' (flying flies) are the floating specks before aging eyes. 'Eine massive Blutung' means 'a severe haemorrhage' and the 'Augenschwester' is an eye-nurse. 'Züri West' is a district in Zurich.

Un posto così / Such a Place
The poem is a dream of a dream, a dream invented by the poet and attributed to his mother, ill in hospital and close to death.

Una delle dieci / One of the Ten
Edoardo Sanguineti (1930–2010) makes this comment in *Postkarten* (Milan: Feltrinelli, 1978), no. 24: 'di un uomo sopravvivono, non so, / ma dieci frasi, forse (mettendo tutto insieme: i tic, / i detti memorabili, i lapsus): / questi sono i casi fortunati' (of a man there survive, I don't know, / but ten phrases, perhaps, (putting everything together: the tics, / the memorable sayings, the lapsuses): / these are the fortunate ones').

Inediti (2020) / Uncollected

L'ignoto di Waterloo / The Unknown Soldier of Waterloo
The epigraph is from of the second movement to Victor Hugo's poem 'L'Expiation' from *Les Châtiments* (1853).

Lezione di scrittura / Writing Lesson
For Fabio Pusterla, see the note to 'Lettera da Binz / Letter from Binz'.

Notifiche dopo l'incendio / Reports after the Fire
Punta Baffe is near Sestri Levante on the Ligurian coast of Italy.

Parlare a una statua / Speaking to a Statue
The work referred to is the *Donna orante* (Woman at Prayer) in the Cimitero Principale of Seregno (the tomb of Giovanni e Luigi Vismara), attributed or attributable, without absolute certainty, to Vincenzo Vela (Swiss-Italian sculptor, 1820–1891).

Su una fotografia di Emmy Andriesse / On a Photograph by Emmy Andriesse
Emmy Andriesse (1914–1953) was a Dutch photographer associated with the Underground Camera Group during the Second World War. The photograph shows a girl in headscarf with a tin dish of anchovies and fishing boats with sails in the background.

Come la pantera di Rilke / Like Rilke's Panther
Rilke's famous poem, set in the Jardin des Plantes, Paris, first appeared in the first volume of the *Neue Gedichte* (1907).

www.ingramcontent.com/pod-product-compliance
Lightning Source LLC
Chambersburg PA
CBHW022010160426
43197CB00007B/361